8 wonders of CINCINNATI

8 wonders of CINCINNATI

WENDY BECKMAN

ILLUSTRATED BY ALLISON RANIERI

THE History PRESS

Published by The History Press
Charleston, SC
www.historypress.net

Cover illustrations by Allison Ranieri.

First published 2017

Manufactured in the United States

ISBN 9781625858986

Library of Congress Control Number: 2017955127

Notice: The information in this book is true and complete to the best of our knowledge. It is offered without guarantee on the part of the author or The History Press. The author and The History Press disclaim all liability in connection with the use of this book.

I dedicate this book to my parents, Jessica and Bob Nielson, who taught me to find wonder all around me and to appreciate books of all sorts.
—whb

To my parents, who introduced me to this wonderful city.
—ar

CONTENTS

ACKNOWLEDGMENTS

I'd like to thank Allison for bringing me into this project. Thanks, also, to Dottie Kuhn for her personal reflections on Ruth Lyons.

—*whb*

Thanks to Alex for all the loving encouragement and support.

—*ar*

Some content was previously published in *Founders and Famous Families of Cincinnati* (Clerisy Press, 2014), *Portfolio* (University of Cincinnati Lindner College of Business) and *Cincinnati Magazine.*

INTRODUCTION

The Seven Wonders of the Ancient World comprised a set of man-made marvels almost too extreme to be believed:

- Great Pyramid of Giza
- Colossus of Rhodes
- Hanging Gardens of Babylon
- Lighthouse of Alexandria
- Tomb of Mausolus at Halicarnassus (from where we get the word "mausoleum")
- Statue of Zeus at Olympia
- Temple of Artemis at Ephesus

In fact, scholars have argued that some of these wonders might be more fictitious than factual. However, whether fact or fiction, only one of these ancient wonders still exists: the Great Pyramid of Giza.[1] So in 2007, based on online voting, a new list of Seven Wonders of the World was announced:

- Chichen Itza, Mexico
- Christ the Redeemer, Brazil
- Great Wall, China
- Machu Picchu, Peru
- Petra, Jordan

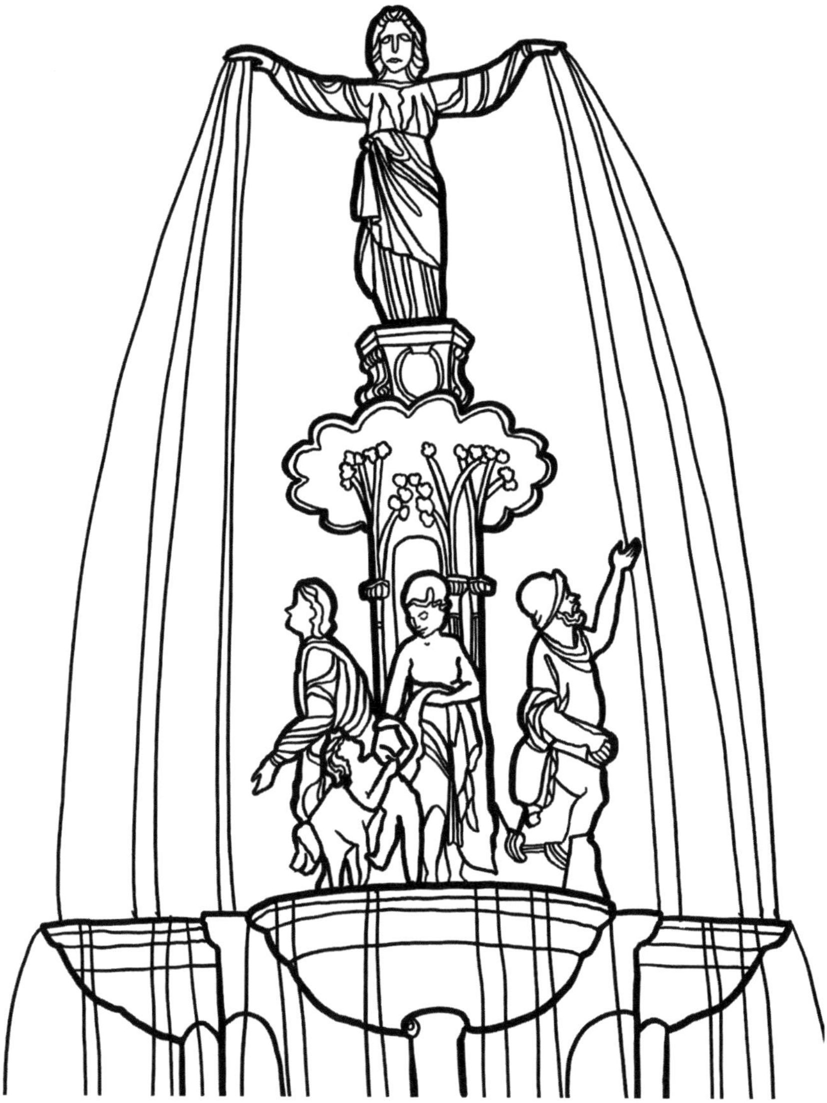

The Tyler-Davidson Fountain, "The Genius of Water," anchors downtown Cincinnati in Fountain Square. *Illustration by Allison Ranieri.*

- Roman Colosseum, Italy
- Taj Mahal, India

These new wonders spanned the globe, instead of being just from the Middle East or Europe. Many other lists of wonders have been developed, including a list of engineering wonders of the modern world and wonders of the natural world.[2] But no one has named the seven wonders of Cincinnati.

Until now.

Not only that, but we also went one further and are declaring *eight* wonders of Cincinnati, representing architecture, art, commerce, customs, food, geography/nature, history and people. Who decided which wonders to choose? We did, informed by your opinions through social media and in person.

One thing's for sure, to paraphrase lyricist Bob Thiele (aka "George Douglas") and George David Weiss: it's a wonderful world. And Cincinnati is a wonderful city.

CHAPTER 1
ARCHITECTURE

CINCINNATI MUSIC HALL

Mention "architecture" in Cincinnati, and two topics come to mind: Art Deco and Samuel Hannaford. Cincinnati was established in 1788, so its existing structures represent the eighteenth through twenty-first centuries. Cincinnati's buildings reflect an eclectic assortment of architectural styles.

Although many world-renowned architects have contributed to the cityscape, Cincinnati's premier architect has to be Samuel Hannaford. Most of Hannaford's work is in the Greater Cincinnati area, although other Hannaford buildings can be found throughout the Midwest, New England and the South. Hannaford created his Venetian Gothic masterpiece, Music Hall, in 1878 to house the May Festival.

Prior to Music Hall's construction, the May Festival was going to be held every other year in its predecessor, Exhibition Hall. At the second May Festival, Theodore Thomas was on the podium. All was ready for the beginning of Richard Wagner's "Lohengrin." Just as the opening notes were played, however, the heavens opened and raindrops thundered on the metal roof of Exhibition Hall. Thomas signaled for the orchestra to stop. (A century later, Erich Kunzel was known to stop performances at Riverbend when racing motorboats violated the "No wake" restriction.) Thomas debated whether he should continue. Finally, the rain ceased and the concert went on.

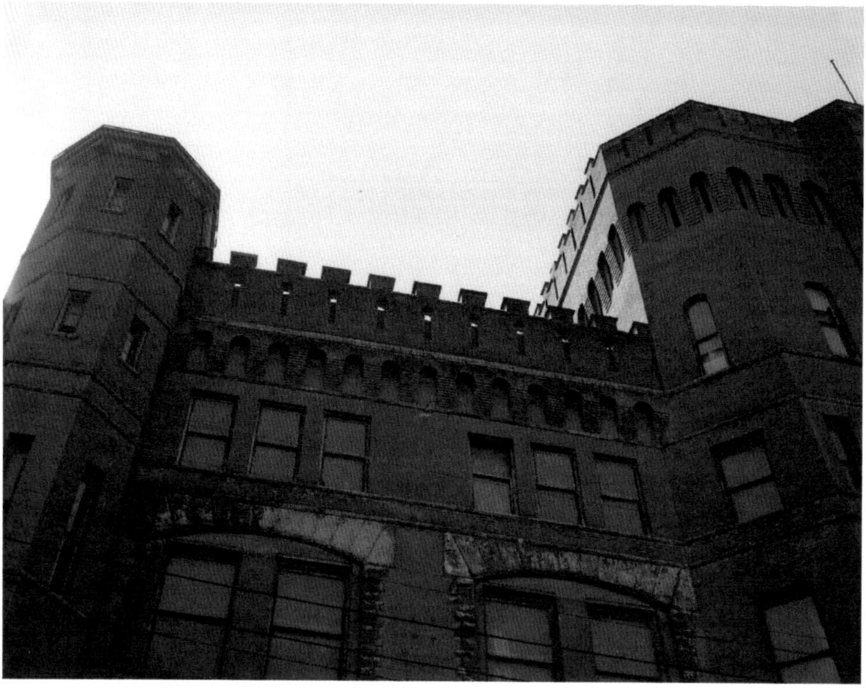

Ohio National Guard Armory, designed by Samuel Hannaford, detail of East Elevation Towers and Parapet, 1417–1437 Western Avenue, Cincinnati. *Library of Congress.*

Reuben Springer was in the audience that night and didn't want a repeat performance from the roof. He immediately proposed that he would put up $125,000—half the cost of a new musical auditorium—if the community came up with the other half. In what might be the first case of crowdsourcing before GoFundMe or Kickstarter came along, Cincinnatians banded together, including schoolchildren donating pennies, to raise the money to build Music Hall. The main performance hall, with its stunning two-ton crystal chandelier, is named Springer Auditorium in Reuben Springer's honor. Music Hall's Springer Auditorium is known for its great acoustics and has provided a wonderful recording studio for the Cincinnati Symphony and Pops Orchestra for decades.

Music Hall, with virtually three separate buildings under one roof, was designed with two purposes in mind: musical activities and industrial exhibitions. Until Cincinnati's Convention and Visitors Center was built in the 1960s, Music Hall served as the city's convention site. It hosted the 1880 Democratic National Convention, nominating Wilfred S.

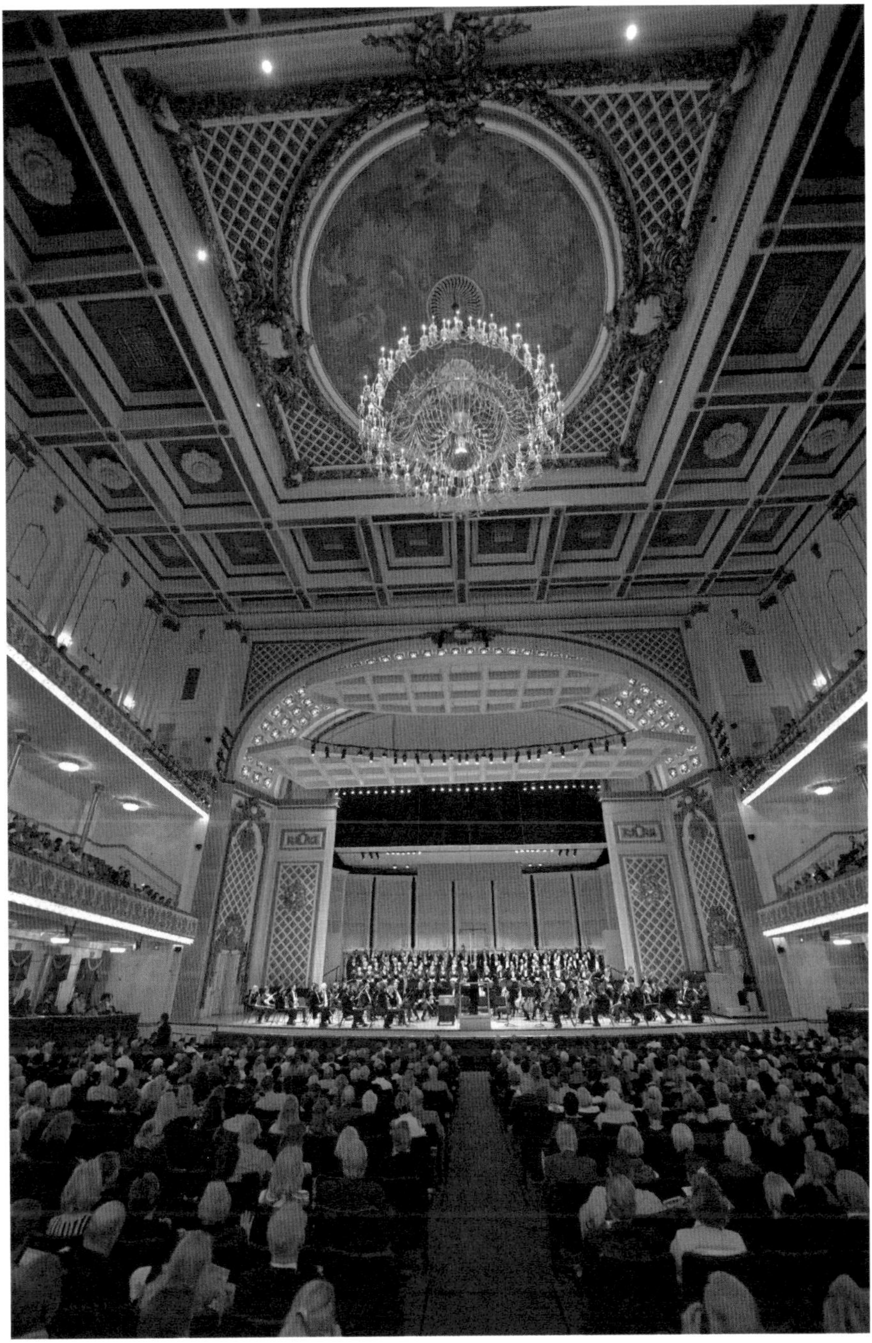

Cincinnati Music Hall, Springer Auditorium, during May Festival 2016. *Cincinnati Symphony Orchestra.*

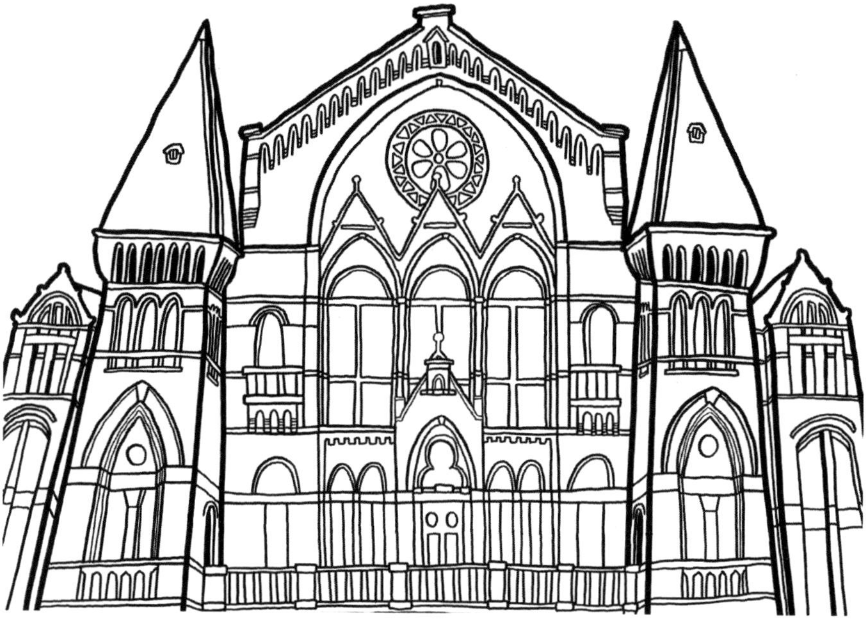

Cincinnati Music Hall, designed by Samuel Hannaford, underwent a major renovation in 2017. *Illustration by Allison Ranieri.*

Hancock. (Its predecessor, the Exhibition Hall, hosted the Republican National Convention in 1876, nominating Rutherford B. Hayes.) The U.S. Department of the Interior designated Music Hall as a National Historic Landmark in January 1975.

In 1876, construction on Music Hall was interrupted when human remains were found. The city refused to have anything to do with the bones. Future president William Henry Harrison, who sat on the boards of both Spring Grove Cemetery and the Music Hall Association, took care of getting them reburied in one plot at Spring Grove.[3]

Fast-forward more than one hundred years, and once again construction around Music Hall came to a stop because of unearthing skeletons. Human remains were again found across Elm Street from Music Hall during Washington Park's twenty-first-century renovation. These bones were supposed to have been relocated ages ago. It could be because people were afraid that they could catch cholera from the bones. Cincinnati had had two bad cholera epidemics in the 1800s.[4] Ghost hunters count Music Hall as one of Cincinnati's prime sites for seeing spectral visions.

At various times in Music Hall's history, it has held a bowling alley, a nightclub and—for a long time—the Cincinnati Ballet. Although the Cincinnati Opera began at the Cincinnati Zoo, it moved to Music Hall in 1972. Along with the Cincinnati Symphony and Pops Orchestra, the Cincinnati May Festival calls Music Hall "home" to this day. A major renovation began in 2016, and (at press time) the CSO was preparing to return to its Music Hall home for the 2017–18 season. The 2017 May Festival was held in the Taft Theatre, with plans to move back for the 2018 festival.

CITY HALL, PLUM TEMPLE AND ST. PETER IN CHAINS

This cluster of dignified buildings should be considered together, for you cannot visit one without seeing the other two. Cincinnati's City Hall is a Richardsonian Romanesque–style building designed by Samuel Hannaford, with four and a half stories and a nine-story clock tower. Hannaford won a contest to build City Hall. Next to City Hall is St. Peter in Chains, the cathedral for the Cincinnati Archdiocese. It was designed by architect Henry Walter under the watchful eye of John Baptist Purcell (then bishop but later archbishop). Built in Greek Revival style in 1845 from white limestone, its 224-foot spire was the tallest structure in Cincinnati for decades. It is the second cathedral, with the original at the current site of St. Francis Xavier church on Sycamore Street. From 1938 to 1957, the cathedral was replaced by Saint Monica's, at the border of Clifton Heights and Fairview. Meanwhile, Peter in Chains underwent a substantial restoration and expansion, under the direction of architect Edward Schutte and Archbishop Karl Alter. It reopened as the cathedral in 1957.

If you go, plan your visit for a time when you can enter the cathedral, as it is like no other in the country. The crucifix is the work of Italian goldsmith and sculptor Benvenuto Cellini. Greek mosaics line the sides of the sanctuary, representing the Stations of the Cross, designed by Carl Zimmerman. Even more stunning and moving is the mosaic in the apse, which was created out of Venetian glass in Aachen, Germany, by Professor Anton Wendling, based on suggestions from Alter. Saints Peter and Paul are depicted, with Christ in the center, above these words: "*Et Petrus Quidem Servabatur in Carcere Vinctus Catenis*," which means "And Peter was kept in prison, bound in chains" (Acts 12:5). The mural is about thirty-five feet

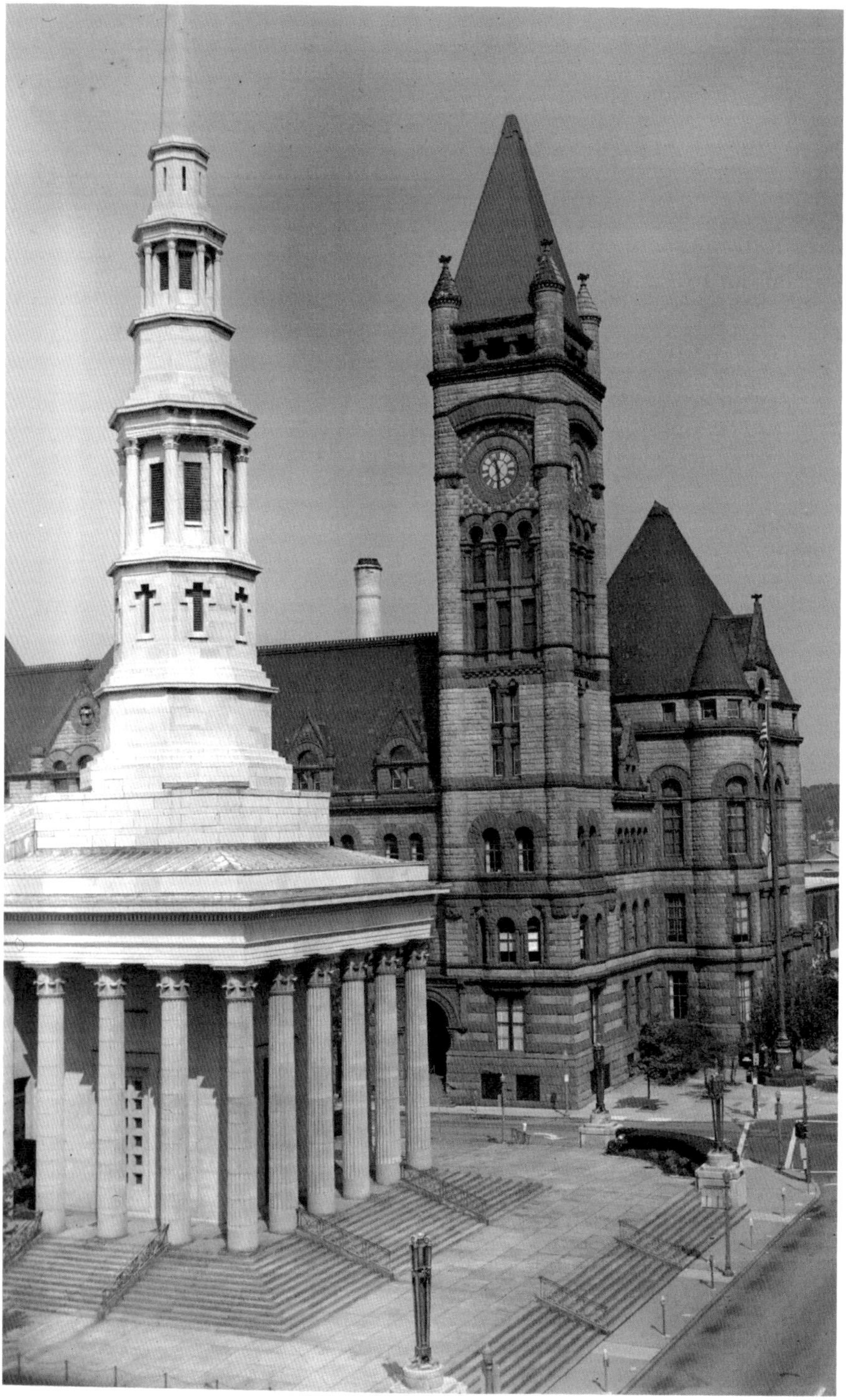

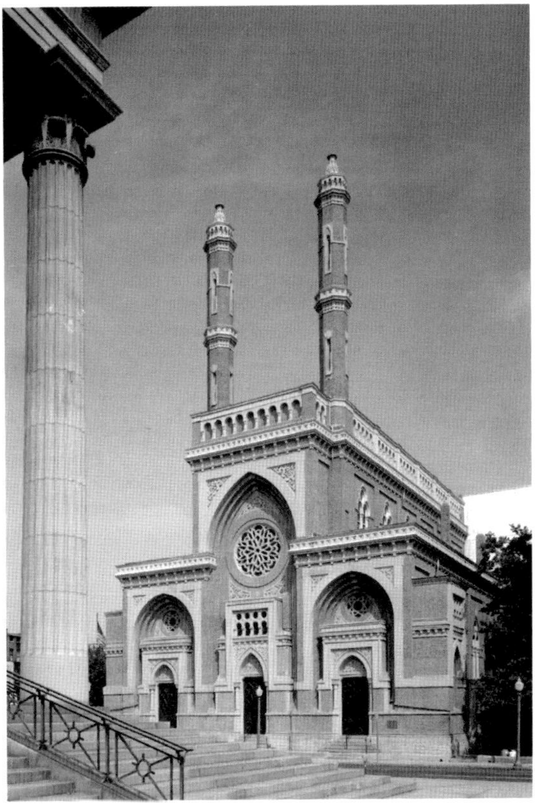

Right: Isaac Wise (Plum) Temple, exterior, with St. Peter in Chains Cathedral in foreground. *Library of Congress.*

Opposite: St. Peter in Chains Cathedral (*left*) and Cincinnati City Hall. *Historic American Buildings Survey, Library of Congress.*

high and forty feet wide and is believed to be the largest of its type in the United States.

Across Plum Street from City Hall and St. Peter in Chains stands Plum Temple. Before the Civil War, twenty-year-old K.K. B'nai Yeshurun was a strong and rapidly growing congregation. Its members procured the land at the corner of Eighth and Plum Streets for $35,000. The architect who designed the temple was James Keys Wilson, a nationally prominent architect. The temple was designed in the popular synagogue style of the day, Byzantine-Moorish, which had originated in Germany. Sadly, similar temples in Germany were destroyed by Hitler's forces.

At Rabbi Isaac Wise's direction, the temple was to hold more than one thousand people. The construction cost was originally estimated at $55,000. Unfortunately, with the Civil War going on to the south, materials and delays—along with postwar inflation—resulted in a final cost of $263,525. The temple was dedicated on August 24, 1866. It is now known as Isaac Wise Temple and is one of the oldest synagogues still standing today.

Carew Tower and Hilton Cincinnati Netherland Plaza

The Carew Tower, at forty-nine stories and 574 feet tall, was the tallest building in the city for a long time. It was created in 1930 by W.W. Ahlschlager & Associates and Delano & Aldrich in a style described as Art Deco and Streamline Moderne. The tower was the tallest until the completion of the Great American Tower (which is about 90 feet taller). Some in Cincinnati challenge the "upstart" that stole the crown (so to speak) from the Carew Tower, as the tallest part of the Great American Tower structure is non-occupiable. The Great American Tower has only

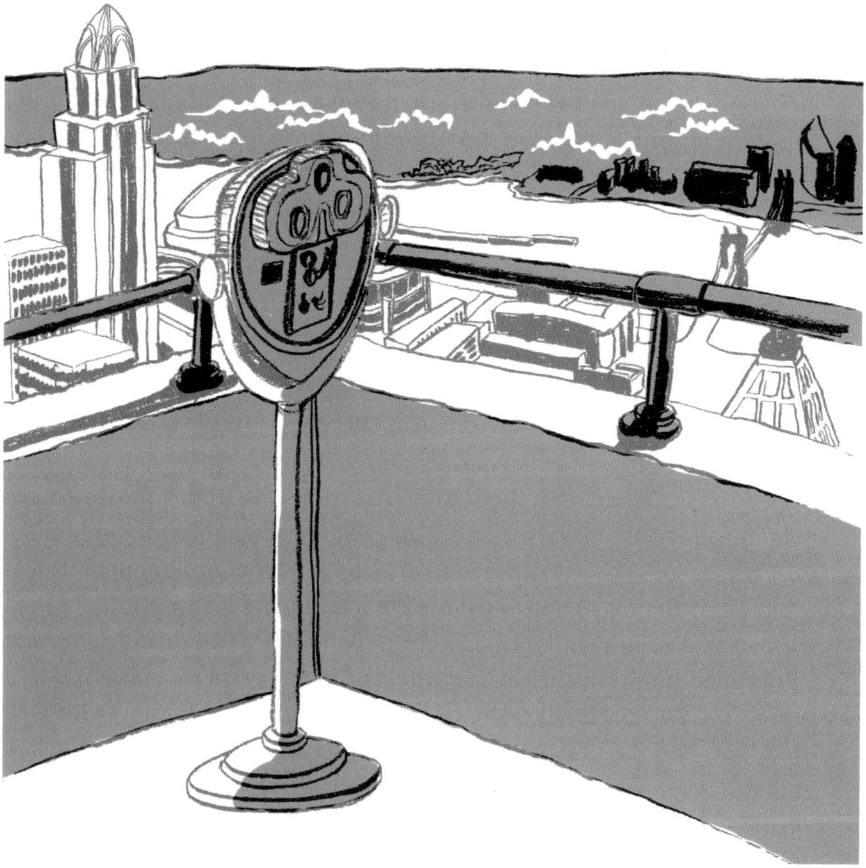

Carew Tower was Cincinnati's tallest building until the Great American Tower (seen in the background) stole the "crown." Carew still has the best view. *Illustration by Allison Ranieri.*

forty-one stories, while the Carew has forty-nine. The Carew's roof is also almost 80 feet above Great American's. However, the best part of this two-tower story is that from the Carew Tower's observation deck, the view of the Great American Tower is spectacular—as is the view of the Tri-State region, including Kentucky and Indiana.

The lower portion of the Carew is 340-million-year-old Salem limestone with black "granites." (They're not really granite.) The limestone came from a quarry in south-central Indiana and contains small, intact fossils of marine animals, as well as some pieces of larger animals.[5]

The Carew Tower was the first building designed for mixed use (even before New York City's Rockefeller Center). Still today, the Carew Tower holds a treasure-trove of goodies. It houses many offices in its upper floors. On the lower floors, you'll find Hathaway's Diner, which is like a trip back to the 1950s. Milkshakes are blended milk and ice cream and are served on a paper doily. Egg salad and tuna salad can be served on a plate or in a sandwich. If you're missing the 1950s, stop in. Also on the lower levels you'll find cafés and other shops. In the arcade in December, you might even find a certain chubby gentleman in red.

The Hilton Cincinnati Netherland Plaza, formerly known as the Omni Netherland (and still called that by some long-term Cincinnati residents), warrants a look, even if you're not in need of lodging. It boasts the beautiful "Hall of Mirrors" for banquets and other festive occasions. Downstairs you'll find the Orchids at the Palm Court, where you can be treated to both delicious gourmet fare and sparkling entertainment. Guests of the hotel have included Winston Churchill, Eleanor Roosevelt, John and Jackie Kennedy, Elvis Presley and Bing Crosby.[6]

POTTER STEWART UNITED STATES COURTHOUSE AND POST OFFICE

Cincinnati boasts a fantastic life-sized collection of Art Deco pieces. Art Deco style, prevalent in the 1930s through '40s, featured clean geometric lines and ornamentation on brick or stone structures. Some of the most famous Art Deco architecture in the world can be found in our humble city. Art Moderne style followed Art Deco, but the two styles are often lumped together. Art Moderne style is similar in structure but without the geometric ornamentation.[7]

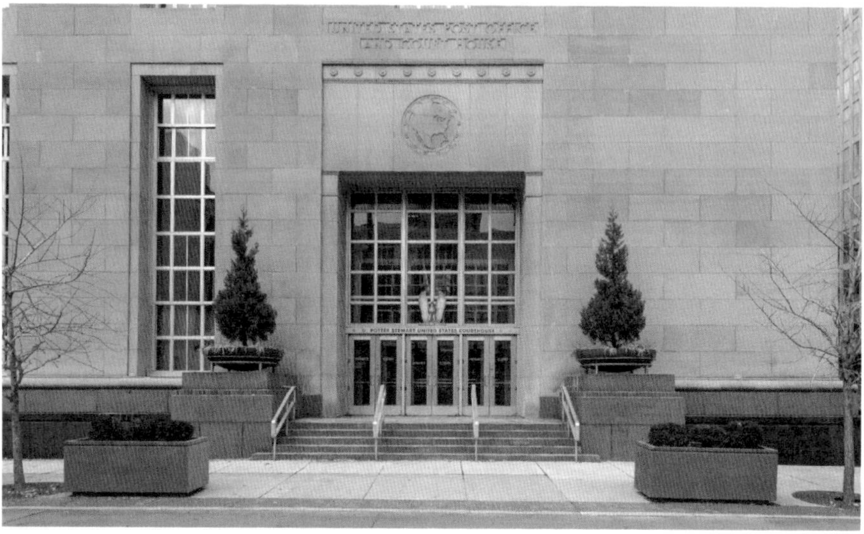

Potter Stewart U.S. Post Office and Courthouse, exterior. It is now no longer a post office. *Carol M. Highsmith, Library of Congress.*

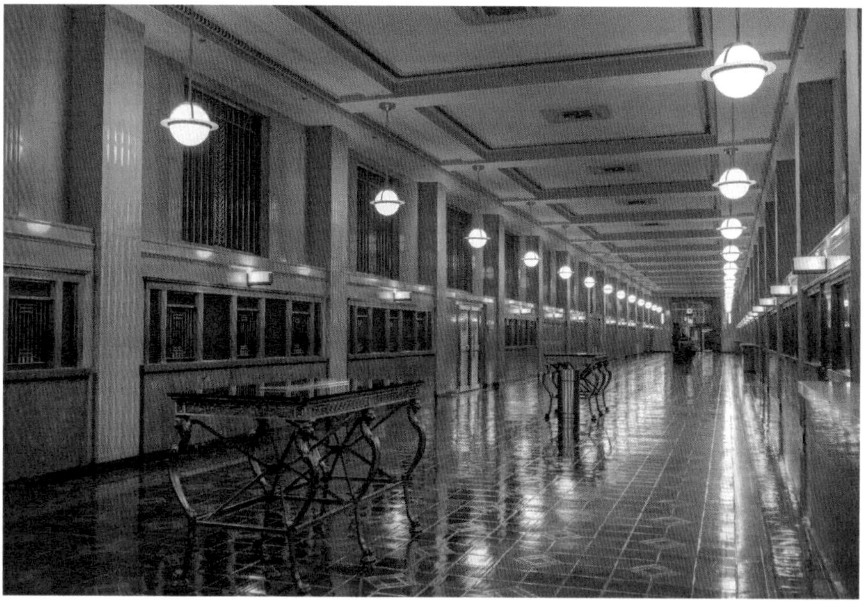

Potter Stewart U.S. Post Office and Courthouse, interior. *Carol M. Highsmith, Library of Congress.*

One building that beautifully demonstrates Art Moderne sits quietly in downtown Cincinnati, in the heart of Government Square. Constructed for just over $3 million, the Potter Stewart United States Courthouse and Post Office was dedicated in 1939. It has a steel frame, and the exterior walls are covered with limestone on top of a dark granite base. The outside is detailed with fenestration bays and a carved frieze.

Inside, you can find two-story courtrooms with the original wood paneling. The two two-story lobbies feature tile floors with marble walls. The building no longer serves as a post office, but it is still the federal courthouse for Cincinnati. Many government agencies are housed on its upper floors. If you want to see these beautiful hallways, be prepared to go through a metal detector at the door.

Potter Stewart was a Cincinnati lawyer who served for twenty-three years on the U.S. Supreme Court after being appointed in 1958 by President Dwight Eisenhower. He served in both the Warren and Burger courts. It was he who uttered a famous statement often attributed to fellow Cincinnatian Simon Leis: "I shall not today attempt further to define the kinds of material I understand to be embraced within the term 'hard-core pornography'; and perhaps I could never succeed in intelligibly doing so. But I know it when I see it, and the motion picture involved in this case is not that."[8]

FOURTH STREET MARVELS

With so many sparkly glass buildings going up in Cincinnati, it might be easy to overlook some of the silent, stony structures built more than a century ago. These buildings were marvels in their day for many reasons. Great examples of these stoic monoliths can be found on Fourth Street.

Thanks to author Erik Larsen, many people outside of architecture know about Daniel Burnham, a nationally renowned architect who was heavily featured in *Devil in the White City*. Burnham was the mastermind behind the 1893 World's Columbian Exhibition in Chicago.[9] What is less well known is that Burnham designed four of Cincinnati's skyscrapers.

The first, the Union Trust/Bartlett Building/Renaissance Hotel, is on the northwest corner of Fourth and Walnut Streets. With its nineteen stories, it was Cincinnati's first skyscraper and the tallest in Ohio when it was dedicated in 1901, a great example of the Neoclassical style. It held the honor for three years as the tallest building in the state until replaced by another Cincinnati building (Fourth and Walnut Centre), also built by Burnham.[10]

The building was for the Union Savings Bank and Trust and was the original home of the Cincinnati Stock Exchange.[11] The building was sold to the Bartlett Company in 1985 and became known as the Bartlett Building. By 2010, it was vacant. Finally, in 2014, the building was purchased and reopened as a Renaissance Hotel (the third in Ohio), with 283 rooms. The on-site restaurant has been named D. Burnham's in honor of Daniel Burnham.

Burnham's other Cincinnati skyscrapers are the Fourth and Walnut Centre (on the southeast corner of Fourth and Walnut), the old Fourth National Bank next to the Bartlett Building and the Tristate Building (on the southeast corner of Fifth and Walnut). The Tristate Building is next to the Mercantile Library, one of the oldest subscription libraries in the United States.

At 1 West Fourth Street stands another Neoclassical structure, the Union Central Tower. The Union Central Life Insurance Company obtained the land in 1911 after a fire had destroyed the former Chamber of Commerce building. Union Central Life solicited designs from architects across the country. The chosen architect, Cass Gilbert, was also in the process of designing the Woolworth building in New York City. The Union Central Tower was the fifth-tallest skyscraper in the world at that time and the second-tallest building outside of New York City. It stands at thirty-eight stories and 495 feet in height.

It was built as a tribute to the classic Hellenic style with its Greek column effect. The lower façade is finely crystalline marble from Vermont. The upper façade is frequently labeled a granite; it is a gray igneous and metamorphic rock known as a granite-gneiss migmatite (from Minnesota). At the steps on Vine Street can be found pink and black bands of feldspar and biotite mica, respectively. Roman travertine from Italy can be found inside. ("Roman travertine" is a brand name for freshwater limestone that was deposited by springs in caves. It was one of the favorite building materials of the Roman Empire.)[12] White terra cotta covers the top, with sculptures representing humans and angry lions. It is capped by a copper-clad temple with a pyramidal cap and aviation lantern. With these touches, many experts feel it is an homage to one of the Seven Wonders of the Ancient World, the Tomb of Mausolus at Halicarnassus.[13]

Union Central Life occupied many of the floors, with Central Trust Bank on the first floor. In 1964, the Union Central Life Insurance Company moved out to a northern suburb, and the building became known as the

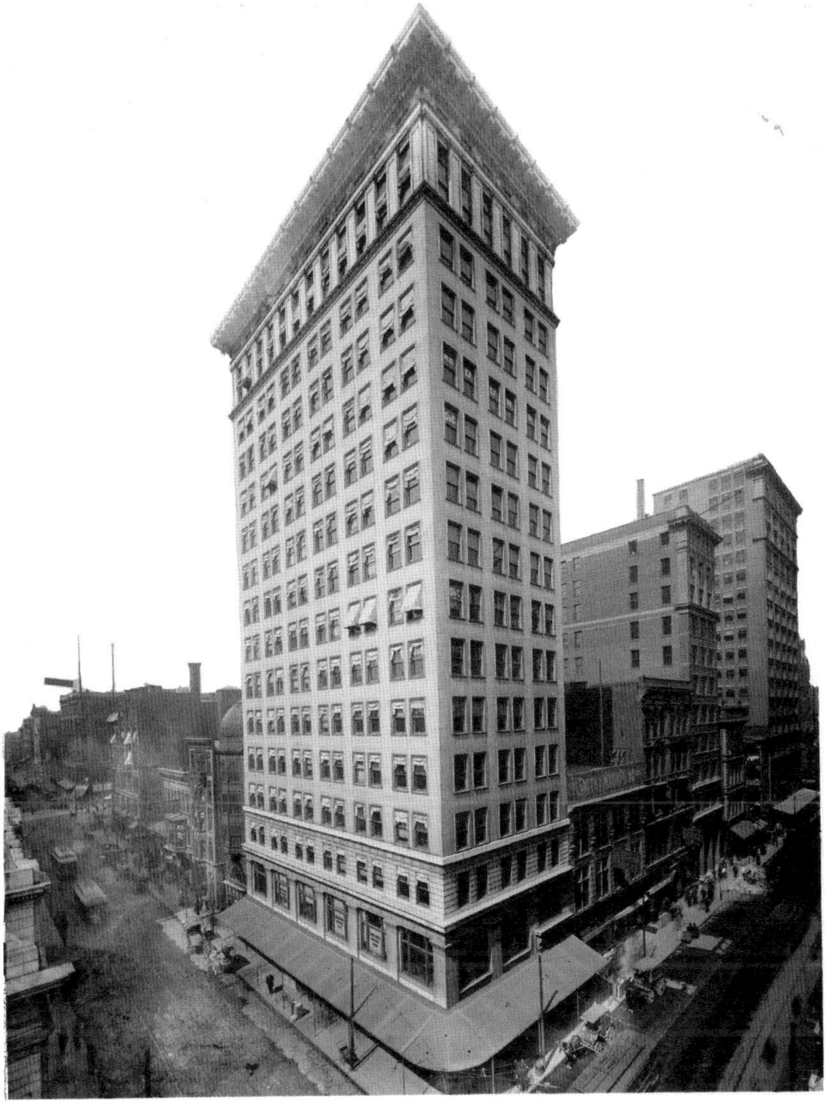

The Ingalls Building, photo taken between 1903 and 1906, Detroit Publishing Co., Publisher. Note the streetcars on Fourth and Vine Streets. *Library of Congress.*

Central Trust Tower. With Pittsburgh's PNC Bank acquiring Central Trust Bank in the 1990s, the building became the PNC building. Its "PNC" atop the tower is a prominent landmark on the Cincinnati skyline.

At the northeast corner of Fourth and Vine stands the Ingalls building. Financed by railroad magnate Melvin Ezra "M.E." Ingalls, this fifteen-story structure was completed in 1903. New Englander Ingalls (born in Maine and educated in Massachusetts) was retained as counsel to the Cincinnati and Lafayette Railroad in 1871, eventually becoming its president. He was president of the Kentucky Central Railroad from 1881 to 1883 and became president of the Cincinnati Northern. He was president of the Chesapeake and Ohio Railroad until 1900, then he served as president of the Cleveland, Cincinnati, Chicago and St. Louis until 1905 and chairman of the board until 1910. The Cleveland, Cincinnati, Chicago and St. Louis Railway was commonly abbreviated CCC&StL and became known as the "Big Four Railroad." Besides his work in railroads, Ingalls also had a strong presence in Cincinnati itself. He was the president of the Merchants' National Bank and the Queen City Club. He co-founded and became president of the Cincinnati Art Museum.

The Ingalls Building was designed by Elner and Anderson architects. It was the first reinforced concrete skyscraper in the world.[14] Vermont marble (a fine-grained, white, Ordovician, 480-million-year-old marble with grayish-green streaks) was used for the first three stories. The Fourth Street entrance has travertine walls. Inside is a cream-colored marble ceiling with veining of gold-black.[15]

Contemporary Arts Center

The Contemporary Arts Center (CAC) has had an exciting past for two very different reasons. These two reasons, however, have the same source: cutting-edge artistic freedom. Cincinnati's CAC is one of the first institutions in the country established to celebrate contemporary art and artists. The CAC seeks to provide exhilarating experiences for all visitors to its exhibits and performances.

The CAC started out as the Modern Art Society in 1939, the vision of three women: Peggy Frank Crawford, Betty Pollack and Rita Rentschler. Distressed at the lack of jobs in the visual arts in New York City, they sought the advice of Edward M.M. Warburg. Warburg, the founder of the American Ballet and the Museum of Modern Art in New York, asked them, "Why not start something in Cincinnati? Plenty of room there. If you decide to try, come and see me and I'll help you."[16]

The three did just that, creating the Modern Art Society and running it from their living rooms. After almost a year, they moved to the basement

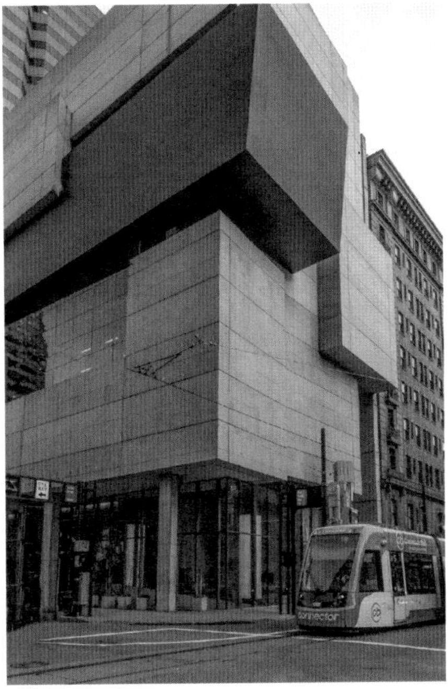

The Lois and Richard Rosenthal Contemporary Arts Center, designed by world-renowned architect Zaha Hadid, with the new streetcar at its feet. *Copyright 2017 RobertMacImages.*

of the Cincinnati Art Museum. They changed their society's name to the Contemporary Arts Center. In 1964, they moved to their own space downtown in the Women's Exchange Building and then again in 1970 to the Mercantile Center on Fifth Street.

It was on Fifth Street that they began to get national notice for being one of the largest spaces devoted to contemporary American art. One especially famous exhibit was that of Robert Mapplethorpe. Some of his "The Perfect Moment" exhibit photographs were criticized for being pornography. Protests, boycotts, a lawsuit and a trial followed. This exhibit, according to the Contemporary Arts Center, "continues to reverberate as much for the artwork on display as for the reactions it inspired and the historic controversy that ensued. Amidst the ripples, then-CAC Director Dennis Barrie was acquitted on charges of obscenity, first amendment laws were shaken and galvanized, the HIV crisis and gay rights movement took on added visibility, and revealing light was cast upon the polarizing politics of what is seen and by whom."[17] The exhibit and ensuing controversy also put Cincinnati on the arts map.

In 2003, the Lois and Richard Rosenthal Center for Contemporary Art was opened as the new home of the CAC. It was designed by the late Iraqi-born British architect Zaha Hadid. Her stunning design, when seen from Sixth Street, was intended to look as if the interior were just an extension of the sidewalk, inviting the public in and wending its way upstairs to its many wonders. The Rosenthal Center was the first museum in the United States to be designed by a woman. The *New York Times*'s Herbert Muschamp proclaimed it "the most important American building to be completed since the cold war." In describing the "stacked cube" effect of the building, Muschamp noted, "I gave up trying to count [the number of floors]. Instead,

I gave myself over to the finely tempered rhythm of spatial compression and expansion that draws a visitor through the building."[18]

Still going strong, the CAC is free and open to the public. Some of the museum's exhibits still might be suitable only for mature audiences, but the UnMuseum provides a family-friendly experience suitable for all ages. The galleries and store are closed on Tuesdays but are open every other day. The Bottle & Basket is open weekdays from 8:00 a.m. to 4:00 p.m. and on Saturdays from 10:00 a.m. to 2:00 p.m.

UNIVERSITY OF CINCINNATI

The birth of the University of Cincinnati (UC) is recognized as occurring in 1819, when Dr. Daniel Drake obtained charters from the state for a Cincinnati municipal college and college of medicine. UC is the second-oldest municipal university in the nation. As the university grew, buildings arose in a cornucopia of styles representing the years of construction.

In the 1980s, the administration of the University of Cincinnati recognized that its buildings, created over the span of almost two centuries, represented a mixed bag of architectural styles. The buildings would never present a consistent image or theme, so university planners decided to have the theme be the diversity of the structures. The university worked with Hargreaves Associates to develop a master plan that would unite and enhance the entire Uptown campus. Issued in 1989, the plan featured "force fields" that split the campus into quadrants, with open lines of green space propelling pedestrians into the heart of campus. Parking lots were removed, and plants took root. The unifying factor of the university's architecture is its diversity. The June 2001 issue of UC's magazine, *Horizons*, revisited the University of Cincinnati Master Plan and checked its progress.[19] Of the many amazing buildings, a few stand out.

The Campus Recreation Center, the work of Pritzker Prize winner Thom Mayne, is a 350,000-square-foot, $113 million facility that opened in 2006. It features a premier fitness facility, campus housing, restaurants, classrooms and a convenience store. The Vontz Center for Molecular Studies, off Martin Luther King Drive on the UC Medical Campus, hosts the cancer and cell biology departments. This signature building, designed by another Pritzker laureate, Frank Gehry, opened in 1999. The Engineering Research Center (ERC) was designed in 1995 by AIA Gold Medal winner and Driehaus

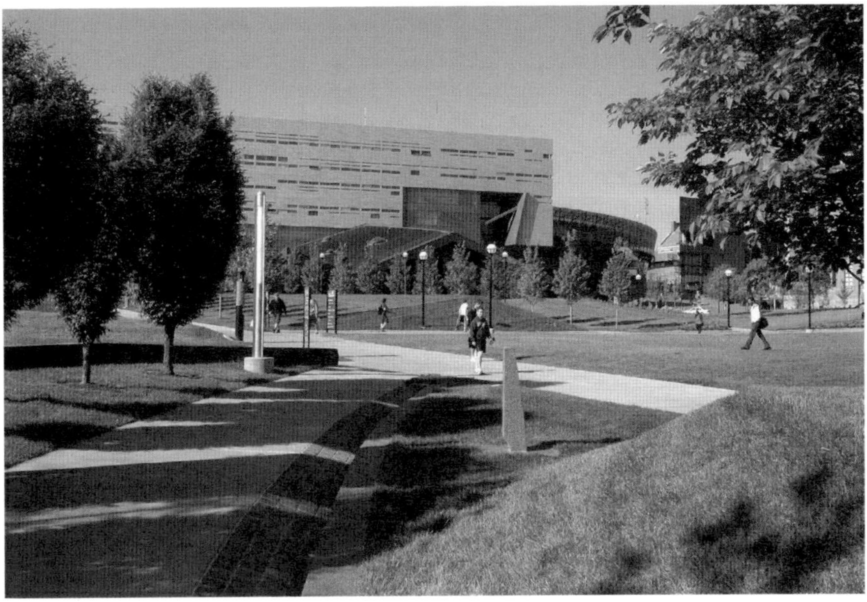

The University of Cincinnati's Campus Recreation Center. *University of Cincinnati Photographic Services.*

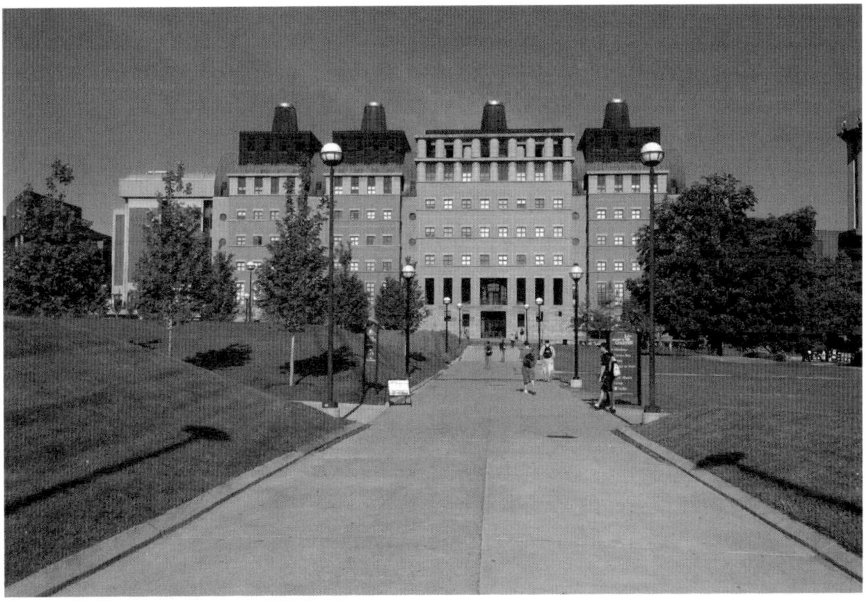

A copper-clad roof crowns the Engineering Research Center, designed by signature architect and University of Cincinnati alumnus Michael Graves. *University of Cincinnati Photographic Services.*

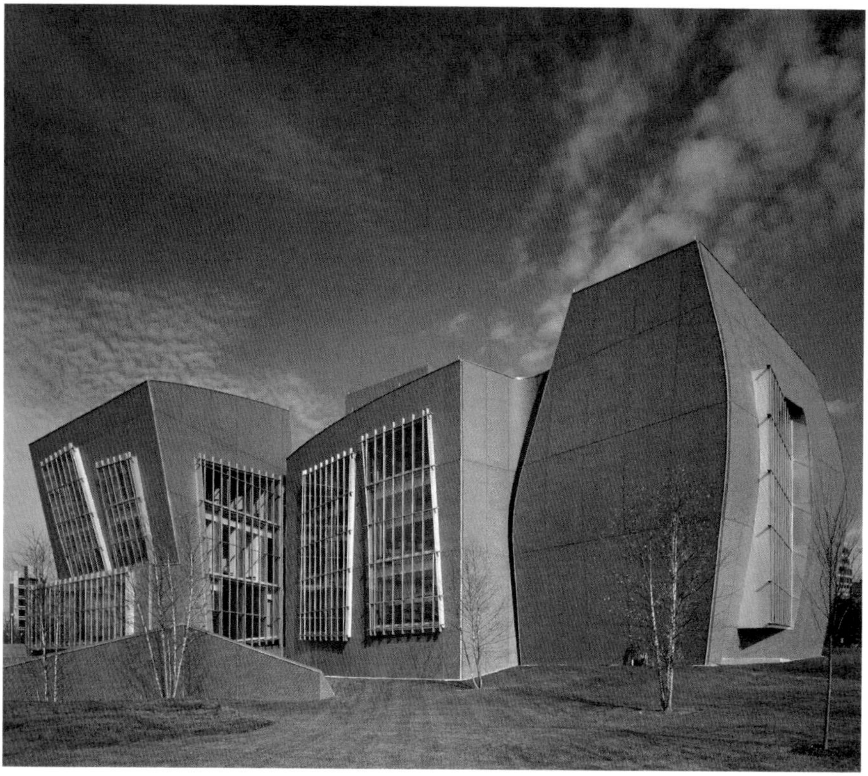

The Vontz Center for Molecular Studies, designed by Frank Gehry. *J. Miles Wolf Photography.*

Laureate Michael Graves, a UC alumnus. The ERC is one of three buildings dedicated to the College of Engineering and Applied Sciences.

The university has received many accolades for its master plan, as well as the individual buildings themselves. In 2012, four of UC's buildings were named among "The 50 Most Amazing Examples of College Architecture": the Vontz Center (described as a "panoply of curved lines"), the Steger Student Life Center ("like a bizarre and wonderful marriage between a curve and the prow of a ship"), the ERC ("eminently pragmatic building in space and form") and the Campus Recreation Center ("a chimera of a building…slammed together in an almost terrifying way"). In 2010, *Forbes* placed UC among the most beautiful college campuses in the world, and a year later, *Delta Sky* magazine named it one of the world's top ten most inspiring campuses.[20]

Union Terminal

Union Terminal is located in Queensgate, on the northwest side of Cincinnati. It was the result of a desire in the city to consolidate the tracks for the seven railroads found in Cincinnati. Construction started in 1928, although the Art Deco half-dome construction began in 1931 and was completed in 1933. At that time, it was one of the largest train terminals in the nation.

The station peaked at 216 trains a day, with some resurgence during World War II. By 1971, Amtrak had taken over, and the trains decreased to 2 a day. Finally, the building was sold to developers, who created an indoor shopping mall and entertainment center called Land of Oz. At its start, the mall had forty tenants, but this soon decreased to nearly twenty. The terminal was closed.

In 1986, the city saved the terminal from demolition with the creation of the Cincinnati Museum Center. It opened in 1990 and recently went through a $200 million renovation.

Amtrak service returned in 1991, with the *Cardinal* making tri-weekly runs. Three days a week, the train runs west to Chicago. Three days a week,

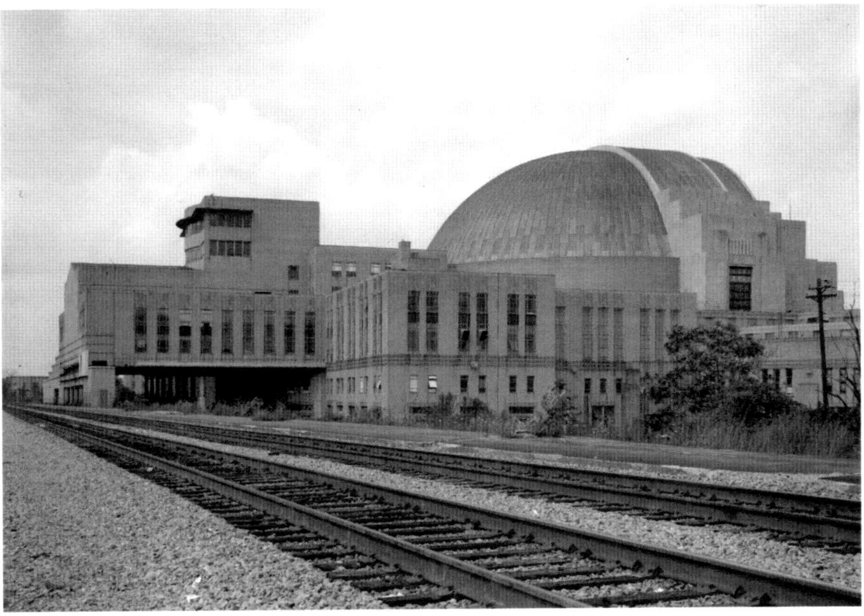

Union Terminal and railroad. *Library of Congress.*

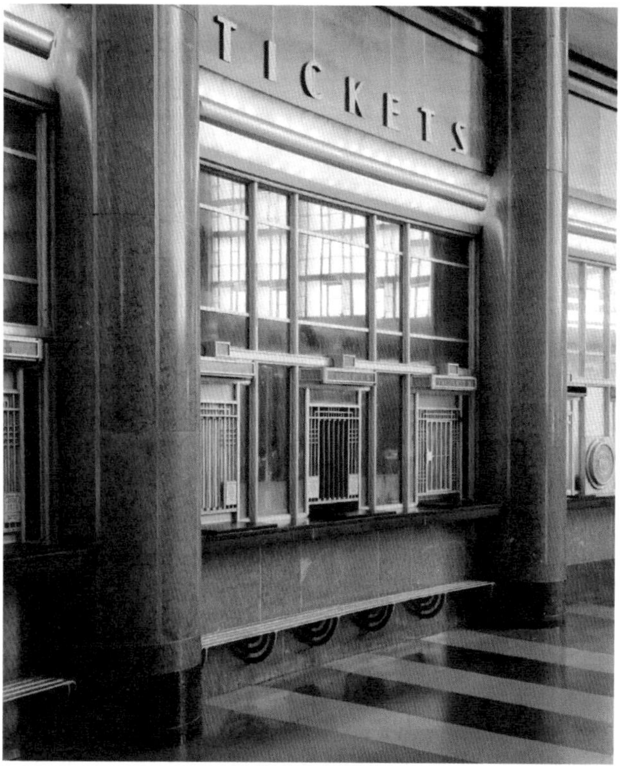

Left: Union Terminal ticket window. *Library of Congress.*

Below: Union Terminal aerial view with Western Avenue. *Library of Congress.*

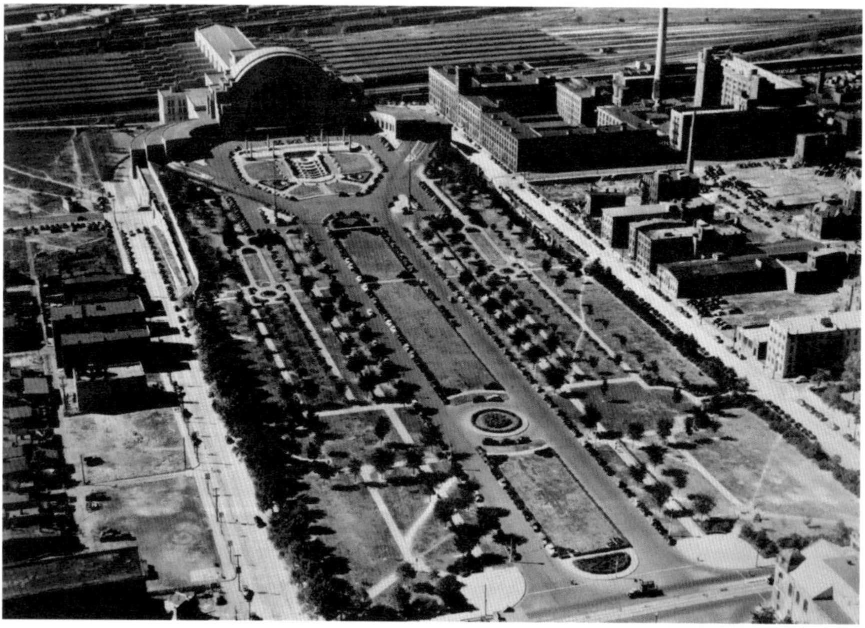

the train runs east to New York City and Washington, D.C. One drawback is that the train stops in Cincinnati in the middle of the night.[21]

When the station was constructed, a series of tiled murals was created by German artist Winold Reiss, each depicting the history of Cincinnati. Two for the main rotunda were 22 feet high and 110 feet long. Other murals were created for the baggage lobby, departing and arriving train boards and the concourse. A large map of the world graced the rear of the concourse. In 1974, when the concourse was being demolished, the murals from the concourse were relocated to the Cincinnati Northern Kentucky International Airport. Only the world map was not saved. When the airport underwent its own construction, the murals were returned to Union Terminal.

CHAPTER 2
ART

Cincinnati Art Museum

Alphonso Taft's oldest son, Charles Phelps Taft, and wife, Anna Sinton Taft, envisioned an Institute of Fine Arts to provide financial support to and help sustain the Cincinnati Symphony Orchestra and to assist local schools in providing music, art and drama for Cincinnati youth. They pledged $1 million if another $2.5 million could be raised. Cincinnatians rose to the challenge, surpassing the goal. The Tafts ended up donating $1 million more.

Thus began the Fine Arts Fund, an annual campaign in support of four local arts organizations: the Cincinnati Art Museum, the Cincinnati Opera, the Cincinnati Symphony Orchestra and the Taft Museum of Art. In 1978, the fund was expanded to include support for the Cincinnati Ballet, the Contemporary Arts Center, the Cincinnati Playhouse in the Park and the May Festival. (In 2010, the Fine Arts Fund was renamed ArtsWave.)

Charles West offered $150,000 toward building a new facility for the art museum, again challenging the community to chip in. Joseph Longworth (son of Nicholas and father of Maria) pledged $37,000. The donors stipulated that the art museum had to be physically separated from the University of Cincinnati. Therefore, the Cincinnati Art Museum was built in the beautiful Eden Park, which had originally been part of the Nicholas (Joseph's father) Longworth estate. The School of Design was then

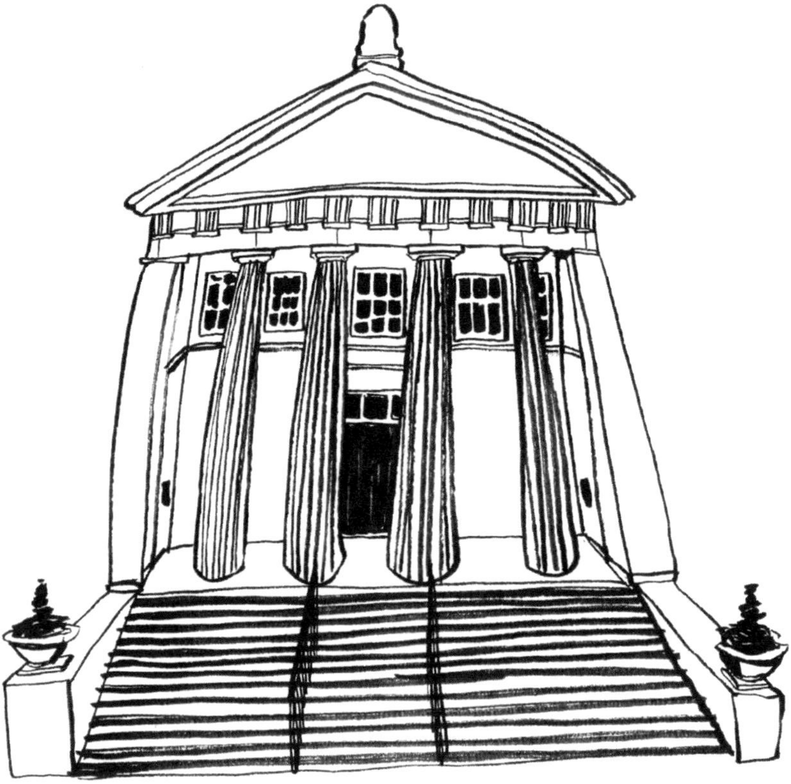

The Cincinnati Art Museum sits aloft Mount Adams in the lovely Eden Park. *Illustration by Allison Ranieri.*

established as a separate Art Academy endowed by Joseph and (Joseph's son) Nicholas Longworth II, David Sinton, Reuben Springer and M.E. Ingalls.[22] It was the first art museum west of the Alleghenies.[23]

Today, the museum has more than sixty thousand pieces in its collection. Although the entire museum merits a visit, the permanent collection "The Cincinnati Wing: The Story of Art in the Queen City" is especially dear to the hearts of Cincinnatians. The wing displays work dating back to 1788 from area artists, including furniture from the nationally renowned Mitchell & Rammelsburg, pottery and tiles by Rookwood Pottery and paintings by John Ruthven, Elizabeth Nourse and Covington's Frank Duveneck.

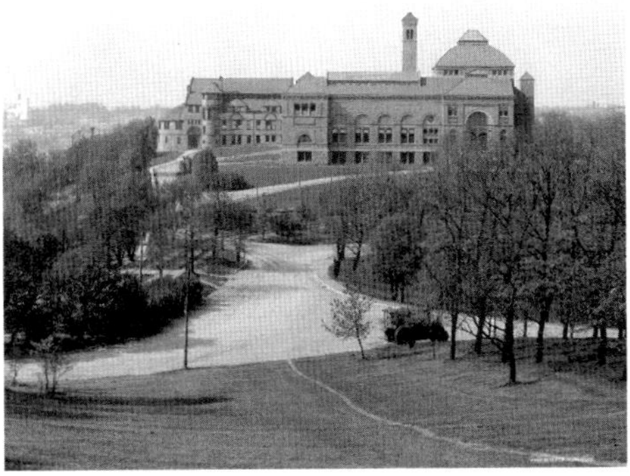

Cincinnati Art Museum, Eden Park, circa 1900. *Library of Congress.*

Duveneck dedicated the last twenty-five years of his life to the museum and left forty of his paintings to the Cincinnati Art Museum at his death.

General admission to the Cincinnati Art Museum is free, thanks to local philanthropists. Learn more at www.cincinnatiartmuseum.org.

TAFT MUSEUM OF ART

Around 1820 in downtown Cincinnati, at the intersection of Fourth and Pike Streets, Cincinnati mayor Martin Baum had a mansion built. He called it Belmont. When Baum died in 1831 from influenza, Nicholas Longworth bought the property. Longworth lived there with his family until his death in 1863, when it passed to his widow, Susan Howell Connor Longworth.[24] After the death of Susan Longworth, the Longworth family decided they no longer needed the sprawling Belmont estate downtown. They sold it in 1866 for $100,000 to a druggist named F.E. Suire. Suire was a wholesale druggist with a store located at the corner of Fourth and Vine Streets.[25] When his pharmacy failed in 1873, Suire sold Belmont to Irishman David Sinton.

Sinton was truly a self-made man, working his way up to becoming one of the chief financiers of Cincinnati Gas & Electric and Cleveland Gas. His only child, Anna, caught the eye of Charles Phelps Taft, son of Judge Alphonso Taft. She married Charles in 1873 in her father's home, the Belmont.[26]

The newlyweds moved in with Sinton, a widower. Anna Sinton Taft discovered that Suire had wallpapered over eight mural landscape panels in the main hall of the mansion. The murals had been commissioned by Nicholas Longworth and were created by Robert S. Duncanson, an African American artist of the antebellum period. Duncanson was a descendant of

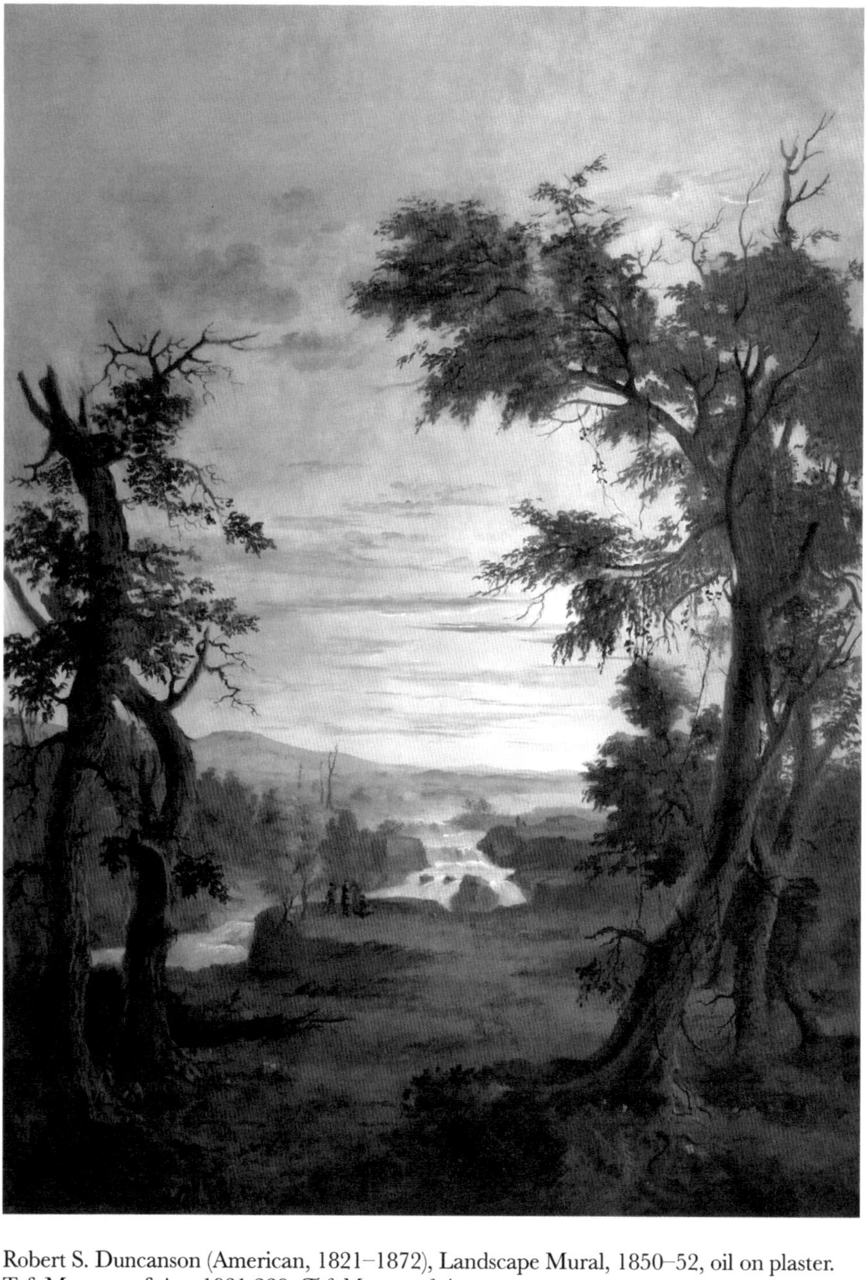

Robert S. Duncanson (American, 1821–1872), Landscape Mural, 1850–52, oil on plaster. Taft Museum of Art, 1931.238. *Taft Museum of Art.*

Virginia freed slaves. In 1842, he had his first exhibition in Cincinnati, but his family was not allowed to attend because they were African American. With the Civil War on the horizon, Duncanson left the United States for Canada and the United Kingdom. His murals are considered some of the best American mural series predating the Civil War.[27]

When Charles and Annie Taft declared their support of the Institute of Fine Arts, they pledged their home to the cause. After their deaths, the Baum/Belmont/Longworth/Taft estate was deeded to the city, including its contents. It became the Taft Museum of Art in 1932 so that all Cincinnatians could appreciate the collections.

Among its collections, the Taft Museum of Art boasts paintings from the European masters, as well as American artists like Duveneck and Farny. The museum has an extensive collection of porcelains and also hosts many traveling exhibits. The Taft is open for admission Wednesday through Sunday, at a small fee. For more information, go to www.taftmuseum.org.

May Festival Chorus and the Cincinnati Symphony and Pops Orchestra

Colonel and Mrs. (née Maria Longworth) George Nichols approached German conductor Theodore Thomas with an idea. They had just attended the Birmingham Music Festival in England. Mrs. Nichols asked Thomas if something similar could be done in Cincinnati. They all felt that with Cincinnati's strong music tradition, it would be a good fit. Thomas and both Nicholses immediately began planning a Cincinnati music festival for the following spring.

They were joined in their planning by prominent Cincinnatians such as John Shillito and Bellamy Storer Jr. (who would later be Mrs. Nichols's second husband), as well as many musicians and members of the Harmonic Society. They planned to hold the first concert in Exhibition Hall. The debut performances in May 1873 received national acclaim. The committee immediately started planning another May concert to be held in 1875. (In the early years, the May Festival was held every other year.)

Twenty years later, the first concerts of the Cincinnati Symphony Orchestra were held, thanks to the wife of William Howard Taft. "Nellie" Taft played a key role in creating the orchestra. Her Woman's Club was devoted to charitable works in support of music in the Queen City. Through the efforts of many, the Cincinnati Symphony Orchestra (CSO) formed—only the fifth such orchestra in the country. When it fell onto shaky financial ground, Mrs. Taft, along with two other Cincinnati ladies, provided $15,000 in funding. They organized the first series of concerts in 1895. Mrs. Taft became president of the CSO and served in this function for many years until succeeded by Mrs. Christian (née Bettie Fleischmann) Holmes, who was then succeeded by Mrs. Charles Phelps (née Anna Sinton) Taft.

The Second World War brought a special kind of fame to Cincinnati's orchestra. The opening notes of Aaron Copland's "Fanfare for the Common Man" are familiar to many. The assertive statements of the timpani and bass drum, followed by the unison trumpets, resonate for many Americans. Cincinnatians might feel a little more resonance than others when they hear those introductory notes, because it was for the CSO that "Fanfare for the Common Man" was composed.

In 1942, CSO director Eugene Goossens wanted to encourage American composers to write stirring fanfares to raise morale among Americans and American troops. Goossens invited eighteen composers and orchestra leaders to compose small fanfares and to dedicate them to the troops with names such as "Fanfare for the Fallen," "Fanfare for the Heroes" or "Fanfare for Freedom." Copland's response, "Fanfare for the Common Man," premiered on March 12, 1943.

"Fanfare for the Common Man" was the second piece that Copland wrote for the Cincinnati Symphony Orchestra. A year and a half before, ten days after the December 1941 attack on Pearl Harbor, André Kostelanetz commissioned three composers to write patriotic pieces to honor great Americans to create what he hoped would be a musical American gallery. Kostelanetz chose Virgil Thomson, Jerome Kern and Aaron Copland. Copland first considered Walt Whitman to honor for his poetry and his service as an ambulance driver during the Civil War. However, Jerome Kern had chosen Mark Twain for his composition, and Copland wanted to avoid using another literary figure. So instead, he chose Abraham Lincoln and created the incredible "Lincoln Portrait."

Kostelanetz and the Cincinnati Symphony Orchestra premiered the works in May 1942, with William Adams narrating. Not surprisingly, "Lincoln Portrait" became a favorite of the CSO and orchestras around the country. It has been performed by many of the world's top conductors and orchestras, usually accompanied by famous narrators. The Cincinnati Pops Orchestra recorded it in 1987 under the baton of the late Pops founder and conductor emeritus Erich Kunzel, with Katharine Hepburn narrating.

The Pops performed it in 1984 and again in 2009, with narrating honors provided by Neil Armstrong, the first man on the moon. As of this writing, the most recent performance was the inaugural weekend for music director Louis Langreé, the CSO's tenth director. The late legendary poet, author and dancer Maya Angelou narrated.

Ohioans are not alone in their love of the work, though. It has been performed around the country and even internationally. Multiple Grammy awards have been given for recordings of Copland's "Lincoln Portrait." Copland and the Cincinnati Symphony Orchestra created two works that went from the heartland of the country to the hearts of the American people.[28]

The Cincinnati Symphony and Pops Orchestra is composed of a core group of ninety fantastic musicians. Many of these musicians also play in smaller ensembles around the city, thus infusing their creativity and spirit throughout Cincinnati.

Cincinnati hosted the World Choir Games in 2012, the pet project of the late Erich Kunzel, director emeritus of the Cincinnati Pops. So in 2012, Cincinnati earned another nickname: "The City that Sings."

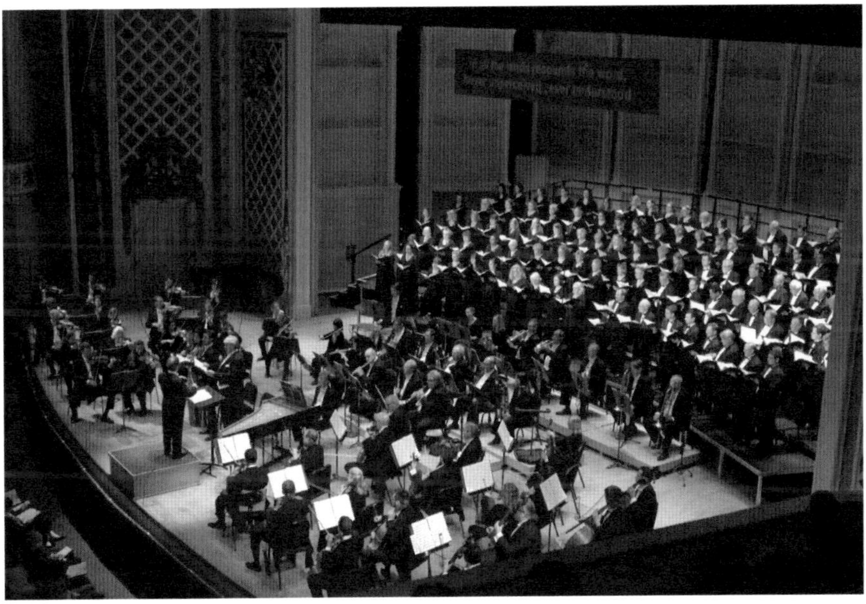

The May Festival Chorus and Cincinnati Symphony Orchestra, James Conlon conducting, May 22, 2015, Franz Joseph Haydn's "Creation." *Cincinnati Symphony/Pops Orchestras.*

Just as Miami University is known as the "cradle of coaches," the Cincinnati orchestras should be called the "cradle of conductors," for many world-class conductors of the country's major orchestras got their start in Cincinnati. One of them, John Morris Russell, returned to Cincinnati to take over the baton at the Cincinnati Pops after the death of founder Erich Kunzel. Two other associate conductors of the Symphony and Pops Orchestras, Steven Reineke and Keith Lockhart, now conduct the New York Pops and Boston Pops Orchestra, respectively. Reineke is also the principal pops conductor of the National Symphony Orchestra at the John F. Kennedy Center for the Performing Arts and the Toronto Symphony Orchestra and the principal pops conductor designate of the Houston Symphony. Lockhart, the second-longest-tenured conductor of the Boston Pops (behind Arthur Fiedler's fifty years), celebrated his twentieth anniversary as Boston Pops conductor in 2015.

The May Festival runs for two weekends in May, but the chorus can frequently be heard performing throughout the entire year as the official chorus of the Cincinnati Symphony Orchestra. The CSO season generally runs from October to early May, when the May Festival takes over. (Here's a secret: the CSO plays for the May Festival.) Then the Cincinnati Opera takes over Music Hall, sharing the space with the Pops during the summer. The Pops season also starts in October but, in addition, has special holiday concerts at Music Hall in December and concerts at Riverbend Music Center in summer. (Here's another secret: the Cincinnati Pops Orchestra is made up of most of the CSO musicians wearing red jackets.) Those musicians are busy!

For more information on the CSO, Pops and May Festival, visit www.cincinnatisymphony.org.

CINCINNATI BALLET

One of the shiny gems in Cincinnati is the Cincinnati Ballet, which has enthralled audiences since 1964. The ballet started with three dance teachers—Myrl Laurence, Virginia Garret and Nancy Bauer—in 1958 when it was first chartered by the Ohio secretary of state as the Cincinnati Civic Ballet. However, auditions were not held until 1963. On March 31, 1963, about two hundred hopeful dancers showed up at the Over-the-Rhine YMCA on Central. The forty-one dancers who were chosen went

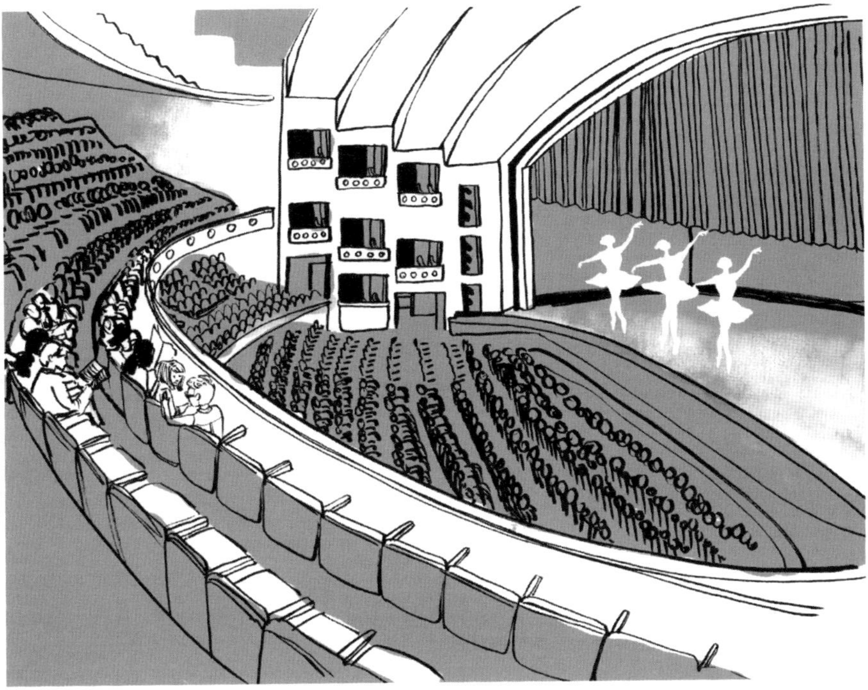

The Cincinnati Ballet moved to the Aronoff Center for the Arts in the early 1990s but will bring three classics back to Music Hall in the fall of 2017. *Illustration by Allison Ranieri.*

on to premiere on March 15, 1964, at the University of Cincinnati's Wilson Auditorium with Oleg Sabline as artistic director.

David McLain, who chaired the Dance Division at the UC College–Conservatory of Music (CCM), was named artistic director. The company began to use CCM studio space in addition to performing at Wilson Auditorium. In 1968, Carmen DeLeone was hired as music director. In 2018, he celebrates his fiftieth anniversary with the company.[29]

From 1968 to 1982, the troupe was known as the Cincinnati Ballet Company. The company began performing at Music Hall in 1978, in addition to the performances on the UC campus. In 1982, it became known simply as the Cincinnati Ballet, which it still is today. Under the direction of Ivan Nagy, the company left UC and performed only at Music Hall.[30]

In the ballet's history, there have been only eight artistic directors. After Sabline came David McLain, who holds the record for the second longest. After McLain passed away in 1984, Frederic Franklin was appointed interim artistic director until the permanent director could be found. Through the rest of the 1980s into the 1990s, the artistic directors lasted two or three years: Ivan Nagy, Richard Collins, Nigel Burgoine and Peter Anastos. Anastos created *Peter Pan*, with original music composed by Carmen DeLeone, for which he was nominated for a Pulitzer. The current artistic director and CEO is Victoria Morgan, who celebrates her twentieth anniversary with the company in 2017—the longest tenure of all the artistic directors.

Except for *Nutcracker*, the Cincinnati Ballet has performed most recently at the Aronoff Center for the Arts. With the refurbishing of Music Hall, some of the company's old favorites will be moving back to its previous venue. Exciting new productions, such as the Kaplan New Works Series, will still find a home at the Aronoff. One of the three that will be presented at Music Hall is the *Nutcracker*, presented by Frisch's. The support from Frisch's, which started in 1974, is one of the longest corporate sponsorships in the history of American performing arts.

To stay *en pointe* with the Cincinnati Ballet, go to www.cballet.org.

Essex Studios and Pendleton Art Center

Two grand buildings in Cincinnati house a diverse array of artists and other creative people. The Essex Studios, located at Essex Place and East McMillan Street in Walnut Hills, provide almost two hundred studios for visual artists, designers and craftspersons and even a church. The artists are painters, woodworkers, photographers, sculptors, jewelers, art therapists,

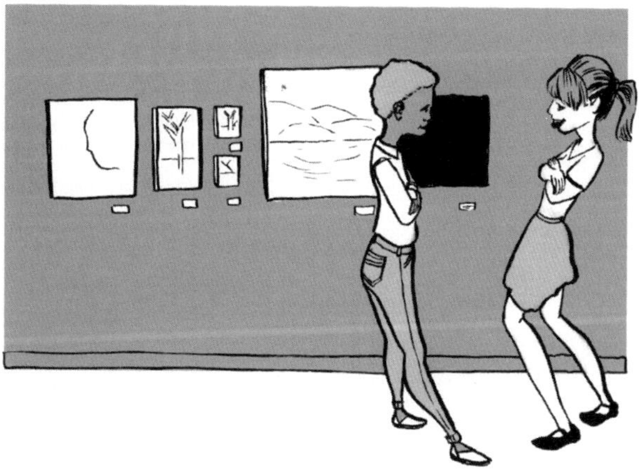

The Essex Studios and Pendleton Art Center present opportunities to purchase artworks and interact with the artists who created them. *Illustration by Allison Ranieri.*

potters and fashion designers, among others. Quarterly Art Walks are offered to the public to allow them to interact with the artists and buy their creations. More can be learned at www.essexstudios.com.

The Cincinnati Pendleton Art Center is located in Over-the-Rhine on Pendleton Street, next to the Verdin Company (the world's oldest and largest bell and clock manufacturer). Pendleton hosts more than two hundred artists on its eight stories. Final Fridays offer the public the opportunity to see the unique artwork, meet the artists and attend educational lectures. Final Fridays are held the last Friday of each month from 6:00 to 10:00 p.m. For more information, visit www.pendletonartcenter.com/cincinnati_oh.html.

CINCINNATI PLAYHOUSE IN THE PARK

For more than half a century, theater lovers in Cincinnati have trekked to the Tony Award–winning Cincinnati Playhouse in the Park, atop Mount Adams.[31] In lovely Eden Park, the Playhouse boasts a distinct view of Cincinnati and the Ohio River.

Cincinnati Playhouse in the Park started out as a college student's vision. Gerald Covell enlisted the help of prominent Cincinnati leaders in business, politics and the arts in 1959 to bring his vision to reality. The initial venue was a shelter house in Eden Park, under the control of the Cincinnati Park Board and destined for demolition. (While attending one production in the 1980s, one female patron was overheard reminiscing about when the bathrooms had been outside.) "Playhouse in the Park" is not just clever alliteration: it truly is in the middle of one of the Cincinnati city parks.

Instead of being razed, the shelter house structure became the Thompson Shelterhouse Theatre, with 166 seats, each offering an intimate view of the stage. The Thompson Shelterhouse's opening production on October 10, 1960, premiered Meyer Levin's *Compulsion* and featured John Hillerman, who went on to success on both stage and screen. Hillerman started a tradition, which continues today, of featuring many prominent actors from theater, television and film.

The Robert S. Marx Theatre opened on July 18, 1968, with *Camino Real* by Tennessee Williams, further establishing the Playhouse tradition of presenting old favorites, while also offering new and original productions. The Marx, designed by Hugh Hardy, won awards for its flexibility and design.

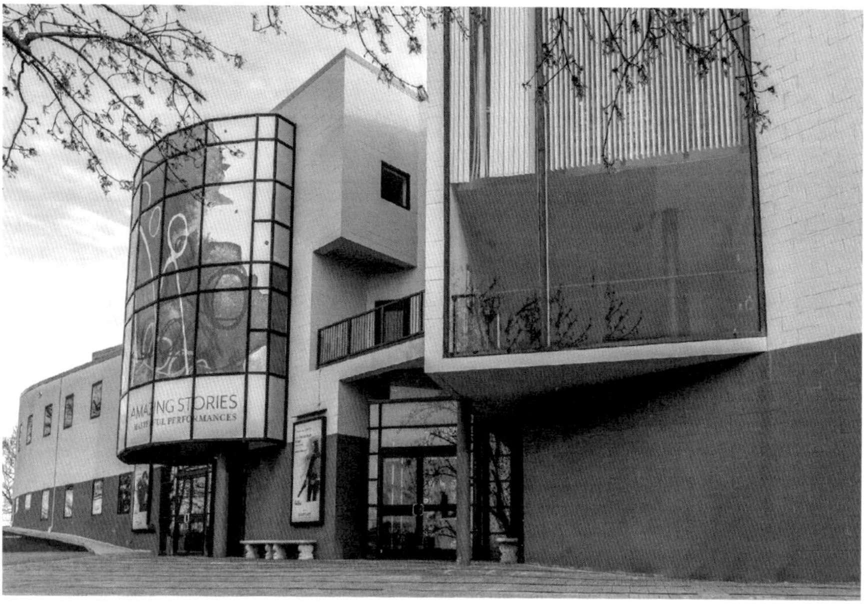

The Cincinnati Playhouse in the Park's Robert S. Marx Theatre, designed by Hugh Hardy, opened in 1968. *Copyright 2017 RobertMacImages.*

With the addition of the Marx, Cincinnati Playhouse in the Park has been able to simultaneously present two productions. The theaters host offerings ten months per year with a typical run of four weeks. Occasionally a play has been extended for a grateful audience.

In addition to its theatrical offerings, the Playhouse also provides a variety of culinary offerings. Themed "Tastings" are offered in conjunction with certain performances, such as a vegetarian spread paired with a nice *Little Shop of Horrors*. Light fare is also available ninety minutes prior to any performance. The full-service bar is available before the performance and during intermissions.

The Playhouse also offers itself as an event venue, with many reservable spaces, including the two theaters. (Of course, use of the theaters themselves is limited mostly to daytimes and Monday evenings.) The Playhouse staff cheerfully helps coordinate the caterers, servers and settings.

Currently, the Thompson Shelterhouse holds 225 patrons and the Marx holds 626. As of this writing, plans are afoot to demolish and replace the Marx after the 2018–19 season. It has not been decided how or where the Marx productions will be held during construction, but the Shelterhouse will probably continue with minor modifications.

For years, moving the Playhouse has been floated for discussion, but the patrons have protested. As a result, the new theater will be built on the footprint of the old Marx. Goals for the new theater include better parking access, more legroom and a new rehearsal room and costume shop. The current Marx stage, which is categorized as a "thrust" stage for the way it juts out into the audience, will be modified with a proscenium arch (similar to the Aronoff or Taft theaters in Cincinnati).[32]

Even with the changes—or perhaps because of them—the Cincinnati Playhouse in the Park will still offer great plays in a great space. For more information, go to www.cincyplay.com.

AMERICAN SIGN MUSEUM

Signs have a special place in many people's hearts. Memories of Frisch's "Big Boy" and McDonald's "Golden Arches" conjure up visceral vestiges of food, fun and family. What happens to these signs when they age or are no longer needed? Tod Swormstedt had the answer.

Swormstedt spent nearly three decades at *Signs of the Times* magazine, considered the Bible of the sign industry. He felt called on to preserve these memories of bygone eras in one place that the public could visit. In 1999, he established the first National Signs of the Times Museum in Walnut Hills. With increasing interest and support, the museum became the American Sign Museum in 2005. However, with increased interest came a larger

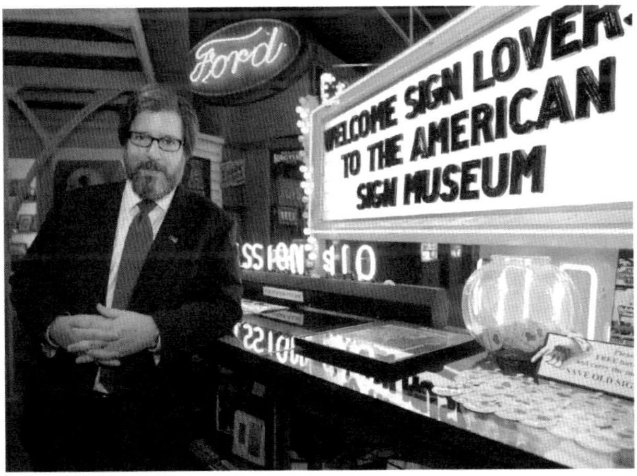

The American Sign Museum welcomes all sign lovers, including marketing professor James "Dr. Earworm" Kellaris, from UC's Lindner College of Business. *UC Photographic Services.*

collection that no longer fit its location—literally. The Golden Arches and Holiday Inn signs were too tall for the environs.

Swormstedt was able to secure another facility, which is on Monmouth Street in Camp Washington, in what used to belong to the Oesterlein Machine Company. The museum relocated and reopened in 2012, with twenty thousand square feet of space. Inside the museum is also Neonworks of Cincinnati, the area's only dedicated full-time neon sign shop. On Wednesday, Thursday and Friday nights, visitors can watch the craftsmen create or repair neon signs.[33] Looking for a sign? Check out www.americansignmuseum.org.

ArtWorks Murals

In 2007, then-mayor Mark Mallory visited Philadelphia and was struck by the creative murals that adorned the city's walls. In the thirty years since its program began, Philadelphia had created thirty thousand murals on what had previously been blank space. Mallory returned to Cincinnati and charged local nonprofit ArtWorks to create murals in each of Cincinnati's fifty-two neighborhoods. Now in its tenth year, ArtWorks has brightened forty-four neighborhoods and seven nearby cities.

ArtWorks's process entails finding blank walls (often through suggestions from community members), gaining permission to paint them and then having an artist create a design that relates to the wall's neighborhood. For example, Camp Washington is the home of a well-known costume shop, so its mural became *Campy Washington*, featuring George Washington in a dress of the period.

An adult project manager oversees the project, which is carried out by a combination of area adults and youth. They've had great success. In 2014, Mayor John Cranley proclaimed October to be "ArtWorks Mural Month" in Cincinnati. At the same time, ArtWorks launched its mural tour program, which is available on its website (www.artworkscincinnati.org). Tours are offered every weekend from May to October, and private tours can be arranged.

Some of the murals depict famous people; some were designed by famous artists. All of them add life to their chosen neighborhoods. One of the most-viewed murals is the *Singing Mural* on Central Parkway in Over-the-Rhine. Designed by local, but nationally renowned, artist C.F. Payne, it catches in

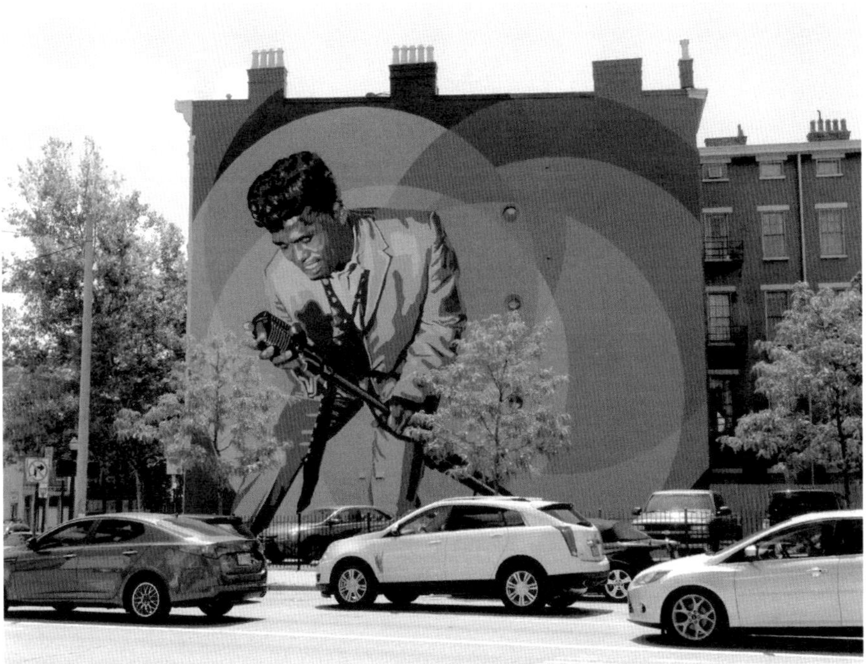

ArtWorks murals have sprung up all over the city, like this one of musical legend James Brown, whose career was launched here by King Records. *Travis Estell.*

mid-song such celebrities as Mr. Red, Mr. Rogers, Erich Kunzel, Leontyne Price and Ruth Lyons, as well as a local police officer.

Love Blooms, on Benson Street in Reading, celebrates the Reading Bridal District—the largest such district in North America. Designer Elizabeth Hatchett highlighted the word "love" for both the ideal and as an homage to brides and grooms. *Garden Party at the Taft* alludes to the works of famous painters that can be found at the Taft Museum of Art. This installation in Bellevue, Kentucky, depicts Rembrandt, Farny and Gainesborough.

The murals celebrate things in Cincinnati's distant and recent past. *Martha, the Last Passenger Pigeon* tips its hat to the Cincinnati Zoo, where the last passenger pigeon died. *Pendleton Mapped* depicts the Pendleton neighborhood, complete with the Pendleton Art Center, the former site of the School for the Creative and Performing Arts and the Verdin Company. Main Street's *Mr. Dynamite* depicts James Brown, whose success was launched in Cincinnati by King Records. Download a self-guided walking tour from the ArtWorks website at www.artworkscincinnati.org.

Chapter 3
Commerce

Procter & Gamble/Porkopolis

For a long time, Cincinnati was known as "Porkopolis" because of its being the leader in the meatpacking industry. As early as 1809, documents detail the regulation of pork packing. Cincinnati had clearly earned the nickname of Porkopolis for its meat processing and products: it was the number-one producer of hog products in the nation. Therefore, it is no coincidence that some of the country's oldest soap and candle manufacturers also got their start in Cincinnati, because besides meat, pigs also have a lot of fat. (An old farmers' adage says that with pigs everything gets used but the squeal.)

Hogs (slow, domesticated fatbacks) and razorbacks (large, fierce and boar-like animals) were walked from the farms to Cincinnati. The proximity of the Ohio River and canal system was a blessing to the hog farmers, because the animals lost about a fifth of their body weight by walking. Cincinnati was treated like a "country bumpkin" in many articles at the time, which described with horror the hog herds in the streets. The hogs were often overcome by the heat until refreshed by fire hoses while on the way to market. Unlike the children's rhyme, none of these little piggies got to cry "'wee, wee, wee' all the way home."

Cincinnati was the nation's top pork producer until the town lost access to the Mississippi River because of the Civil War. Also, because of its wonderful waterways, Cincinnati had been late in jumping on the railroad

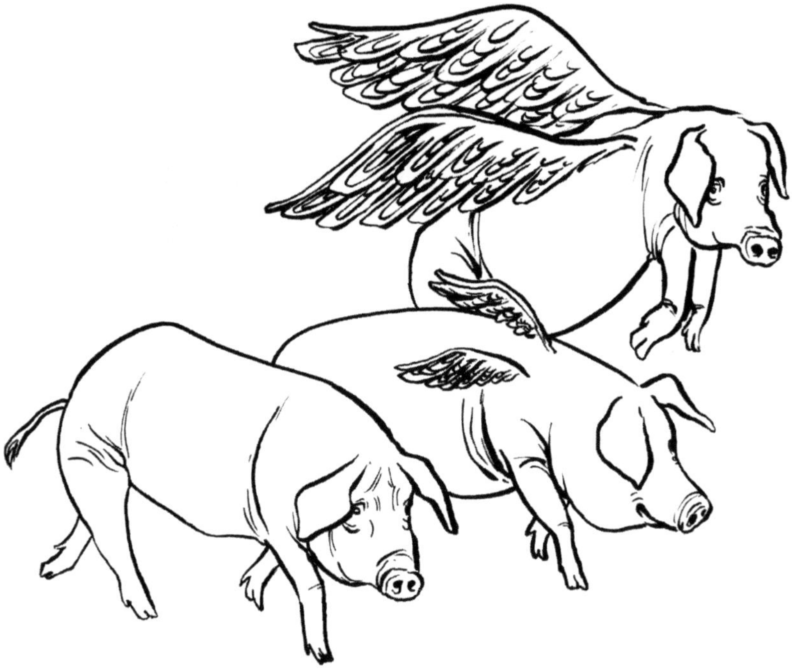

In Porkopolis, pigs worked off many calories walking to market. *Illustration by Allison Ranieri.*

bandwagon. Chicago usurped Cincinnati's position as meatpacking leader. But in its heyday of the 1830s and 1840s, Cincinnati was processing more than eighty-five thousand hogs a year in more than twenty-five meat plants.[34]

World history was changed when an English candle maker named William Procter immigrated to the United States in the early 1800s, after his London dry goods shop was robbed. Procter's wife became ill and died soon after they arrived in Cincinnati. Procter, however, had found a good home here. He got a job at a bank and practiced his candle-making on the side. Through his candle-making, he was able to pay off the debt he had incurred because of the robbery. Soon Procter left the bank to make candles full time. He also began courting Olivia Norris, a daughter of Alexander Norris, a prominent candle maker from Ireland.

James Gamble followed a similar path. The Gambles were struggling in Ireland, in the newly formed United Kingdom. Facing overpopulation, a major depression and rampant disease, many Irish people emigrated. In 1819, the Gamble family came to the United States, planning on going to

Illinois. James, who was sixteen years old, became ill, forcing the family to stop in Cincinnati. By the time James recovered, the family had decided to stay in Cincinnati. James became an apprentice to a man who made soaps and candles, eventually becoming a soap and candle maker in his own right. He married Elizabeth Ann Norris, thus becoming a brother-in-law to William Procter.

Alexander Norris was frustrated that his two sons-in-law were competing against each other for resources, so he tried to convince the two to become partners. After years of nagging, he finally succeeded.

William Procter and James Gamble became partners on October 31, 1837, creating the Procter & Gamble Company. They began by creating and selling soaps and candles. Gamble made the soaps and candles, and Procter made the sales. Procter filled a wheelbarrow with their products and walked them to stores. When their business grew, they moved to a location on Western Row (now called Central Avenue), closer to the slaughterhouses and their tallow supply.[35]

By the end of the decade, James Gamble and William Procter had been joined by Michael Werk from Alsace, Thomas Emery from England and Andrew Jergens from Germany, who started using the abundant fats and oils of Porkopolis to establish their own soap and candle empires. Soon Cincinnati's soaps were sold throughout the state.

About a decade after the Civil War, a worker at Procter & Gamble had a happy accident. Cincinnati legend has it that he left the blending machine running on a batch of white soap while he went to lunch. At first they thought they would discard the resulting batch of hard soap, which could float. Rather than wasting it, however, they sold it anyway. The buyers loved it and wanted more.

William Procter's son Harley wanted to market it separately from their regular white soap, but he needed a name for it. He later related that he was sitting in church one Sunday when he read Psalm 45:8: "All thy garments smell of myrrh, and aloes, and cassia, out of the ivory palaces, whereby they have made thee glad." Suddenly, he had his name for the new soap: Ivory! After Thomas Alva Edison's invention of the electric light bulb in 1879, candle sales declined, but P&G's soap sales kept it afloat.[36]

Today, P&G is a global corporation and owns many other companies. Its Ivory soap division was spun off as the St. Bernard Soap Company, named for the neighborhood in which it is located. The original Ivorydale building is still partially occupied by P&G, as well as J.M. Smucker Company (which makes Crisco there).

United Dairy Farmers/ American Financial Group

Cincinnati played a leading role in solving a national health problem. In the late 1800s and early 1900s, purity of milk was being examined. Health laws required testing of raw milk before it left the farm; some dairies tested both their raw and pasteurized milk.

Then in 1906, physicians in Cincinnati established a milk commission and called for a national conference on milk safety. On June 3, 1907, in Atlantic City, those gathered established the American Association of Medical Milk Commissions. One concern raised was the number of infants and children who died from what was often called "summer complaint" (identified also in historical documents as being cholera or severe gastroenteritis). "Summer complaint" sounds like a minor irritant, but it was a fatal, severe diarrhea accompanied by fever and vomiting. Doctors often blamed milk that had not been kept cool while being delivered from horse-drawn milk wagons. The problem wouldn't be solved right away, but it was a group of Cincinnatians once again that came up with the solution.

In the late 1930s, most milk was still delivered directly to homes. Prior to the 1930s, milkmen rode horse-drawn wagons to each house, where each customer would indicate how many bottles she wanted that day. In those days, often if the housekeeper or mistress of the house was not home, the milkman would put the milk in her icebox for her. Sometimes the milk was left in a small box on the back step.

Between 1932 and 1936, most local dairies stopped using horse-drawn milk wagons in favor of motorized trucks. However, milkmen often did not sell all the milk they carried in the truck, whether powered by horse or engine. Milk that came back at the end of the day had to be tested to see if it was still suitable for use. Some "returns" were processed to separate out the fat and make butter with it.

Carl Henry Lindner came up with an idea in 1938 to offer dairy products on a "cash-and-carry" basis in his Norwood store. His milk was not being carried around on milk wagons all day, so less milk was spoiled, which reduced his costs. He also had no delivery costs, so he could offer his milk and dairy products at lower prices. Of course, part of Lindner's challenge was convincing housewives that the lower-priced cold milk was worth their inconvenience of getting it from the store.

Lindner's sales on the first day of business amounted to $8.28. When Lindner closed the store that night, two milkmen—upset at the competition

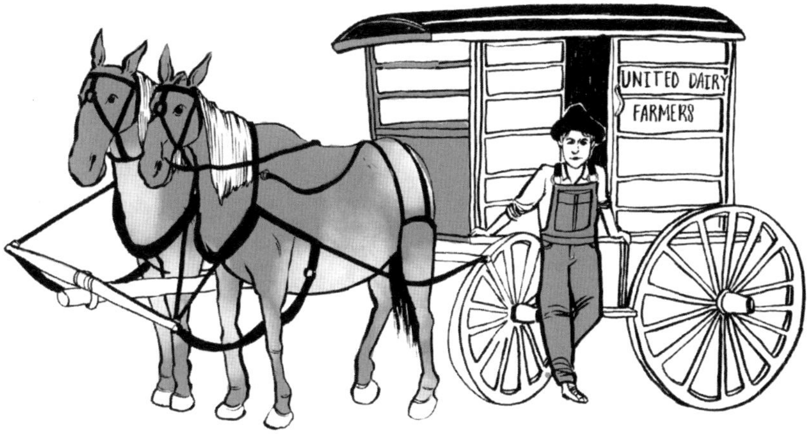

Carl Lindner's idea for a "cash-and-carry" dairy store meant milk no longer had to be carried around on wagons all day. *Illustration by Allison Ranieri.*

their wagons would face—met him at the back door and beat him up. Lindner Sr., along with his three sons and daughter (Carl, Robert, Richard and Dorothy), was not to be scared off. United Dairy Farmers (UDF) was in the milk business for good.

Carl Lindner's health got worse in the early 1950s, so Carl Jr. assumed leadership of UDF. When Carl Sr. died in 1952, UDF had eleven stores. Six years later, this number had doubled.

After a while, Carl Lindner Jr. turned over the helm of UDF to his younger brother Robert while he turned his own attention to American Financial Corp., a company he had founded in 1959. Carl Lindner Jr. began acquiring other local businesses. At one point, he controlled Great American Insurance Company, Provident Financial Group, Chiquita Brands, the Cincinnati Reds, the *Cincinnati Enquirer*, Thriftway and Bantam Books, among others. From 1999 to 2005, Carl Lindner Jr. was the majority owner of the Cincinnati Reds ball club. In 2005, he sold the team to Bob Castellini but maintained a minority ownership until his 2011 death.

The Lindners' largesse reached far as well. Carl was a generous supporter of the Cincinnati Pops Orchestra and the May Festival, the Cincinnati Zoo's Center for Reproduction of Endangered Wildlife (CREW) and the Ice

Age Exhibit at the Cincinnati Museum Center. Robert Lindner supported the Robert D. Lindner Family Omnimax Theater, also at the Cincinnati Museum Center. Richard's generosity created the Richard E. Lindner Varsity Village on the University of Cincinnati Uptown Campus. In 1989, the Lindners founded a school, the Cincinnati Hills Christian Academy, a private Christian K–12 school north of Cincinnati.

In 2005, a $30 million gift from the Craig and Frances Lindner and Edyth and Carl H. Lindner Jr. families established the Craig and Frances Lindner Center of HOPE (Helping Other People Excel) in Mason, Ohio, just north of Cincinnati. One of the newest freestanding mental health centers in North America, the Lindner Center of HOPE is operated jointly by the University of Cincinnati Department of Psychiatry, UC Health and the Lindner Foundation. The Lindner Center of HOPE provides outpatient and inpatient services for adults and adolescents eleven years and older. It is yet one more way in which the Lindner families have cared for the Cincinnati community.

After years of Carl Lindner's magnanimous support, the University of Cincinnati named its College of Business for Lindner just three months before he died in October 2011 at the age of ninety-two. Carl Lindner's drive and generosity are continued in the hands of his three sons, Carl III, Craig and Keith.

READING BRIDAL DISTRICT

Every year, thousands of brides and their attendants flock to Reading, just north of Cincinnati. Along Benson Street is the Reading Bridal District, the largest such district in North America.

The district started out with Bride & Formal opening its doors in 1979. Bridal & Formal started with two employees and a handful of gowns. Now it employs more than fifty associates, and its shelves hold thousands of gowns. Other stores followed suit. Today, the district is said to have more than nine thousand bridal gowns. Benson Street is a one-stop shop for brides and their families. Within a two-mile radius, blushing brides can find a dozen gown stores and five photography studios, plus caterers, cake makers, venues, musicians, event planners, florists—and even a bank.

Reading is not just for brides, though: mothers, attendants, flower girls and even prom-goers can find the gown of their dreams without even moving the car. For the wedding of your dreams, visit www.readingbridaldistrict.com.

KROGER

In the 1870s, one of the worst financial panics hit the country with the failure of Jay Cooke and Company, the bank that had funded the Northern Pacific Railroad. Although the country recovered about five years later, thousands of businesses had failed, including many banks and railroads. However, at least one business got its start despite the tragedy.

Bernard Henry Kroger's father emigrated from Germany and opened a dry goods store in Covington, Kentucky, across the river from Cincinnati. The financial Panic of 1873 cost Kroger everything he had—including his life. His thirteen-year-old son, nicknamed Barney, started working to make ends meet for the family of twelve. However, Barney's mother did not approve of his working on the Sabbath. He finally found a job working for the Great Northern and Pacific Tea Company and sold coffee and tea door to door.

Barney Kroger found he had a talent in food retail and soon worked his way into management, finally establishing his own store. When Kroger was twenty-three, he and a friend, B.A. Branagan, established the Great Western Tea Company in 1883. Misfortune arrived in their first year, however, when their new horse and cart, driven by Branagan, collided with a train. Branagan survived, but the cart and horse were destroyed. Then one of Cincinnati's many floods destroyed their entire inventory. Nevertheless, they turned a profit by the end of their first year, and Kroger bought out Branagan's share. Then in 1884, he bought a second store.

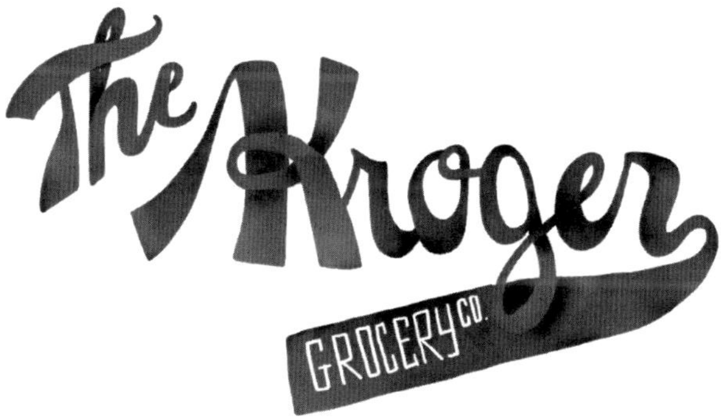

Barney Kroger's logo soon became familiar to people throughout the Midwest. *Illustration by Allison Ranieri.*

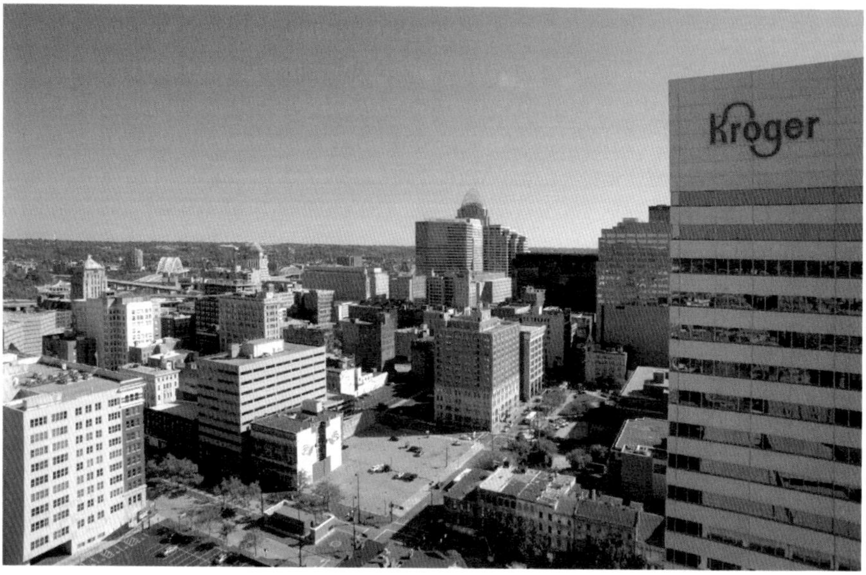

The Kroger building shows how far the company has come from Barney Kroger's humble beginnings. *Travis Estell.*

Financial panics haunted Kroger all his life. Like that of 1873, another panic had a profound effect on him. When the Panic of 1893 hit, Kroger felt sure that his bank would not fail. He left his money in the bank.

When many Cincinnati businesses succumbed, Kroger bought them up. When the crisis was over, he owned seventeen stores. By the turn of the century, he had changed how consumers shopped. Because he owned so many stores, he could buy items in bulk and sell them at a lower price. He established bakeries and butcheries in his stores, offering fresh-baked goods and meats. Kroger offered his customers lower prices and created the convenience of one-stop shopping.

By the twentieth century, it was obvious to many that Barney Kroger was a successful food retailer. What was less known was that he was also generous, often making magnanimous, anonymous donations. In one instance, he asked a *Cincinnati Post* journalist to bring him a person who could use financial assistance. The reporter brought Kroger a young doctor who was working with tuberculosis patients; Kroger wrote the doctor a check for $6,000. In 1911, Kroger worked with Frances Pollak and others to establish the Cincinnati Association for the Blind (now known as the Cincinnati Association for the Blind and Visually Impaired) to assist people with visual disabilities in getting access to job training and education.[37]

MARIA LONGWORTH AND ROOKWOOD POTTERY

Maria Longworth played an essential role in founding a musical festival, the Cincinnati May Festival, and in the construction of Music Hall itself. She is better known—internationally—for being the first woman to operate a manufacturing business: Rookwood Pottery.

Maria Longworth had long been thrilled with art and the craft of painting pottery. Longworth was offended when she thought she had not received an invitation to join a ladies' pottery club in Cincinnati. They swore they had sent the invitation; she just hadn't received it. Not to be assuaged, Longworth started her own group. In 1876, she exhibited her work at Philadelphia's Centennial Exposition. In 1879, she commissioned the building of a special kind of pottery kiln for the type of painting she was doing. Her father, Joseph, purchased an old building, which he turned into a studio for her creations, and thus Rookwood Pottery was born in 1880, named for her grandfather's estate.

Maria Longworth Nichols's Rookwood Pottery experienced great success. It was known for its potters' skills as well as its pottery glazes. She transferred her interest in the company in 1883 to William W. Taylor, the business manager. Under Taylor also, the company flourished.

Unfortunately, first the Great Depression and then the atmosphere leading up to the Second World War had a profound effect on sales. The company

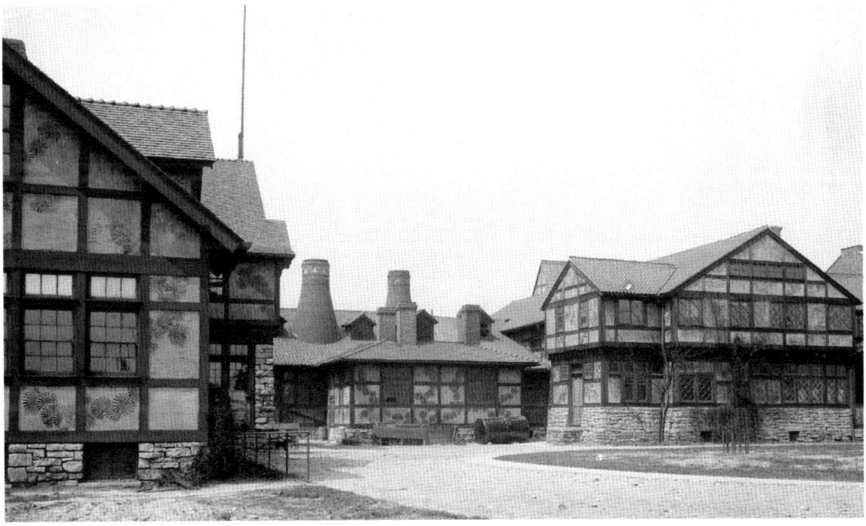

Rookwood Pottery in one of its many former lives. Converted from a warehouse to a pottery barn, in recent decades it has usually held a restaurant. It's currently closed. *Library of Congress.*

closed shop in 1941. However, a group of investors led by Walter E. Schott and his wife, Margaret, bought the company in the 1940s and started production again. The company changed hands many times through the '50s and '60s, landing in the hands of the Herschede Clock Company until closing again in 1967. In 1982, a dentist, Arthur Townley, and his wife, Rita, bought Rookwood—including all the molds, tiles and trademark glazes—because of their long standing as collectors. Sadly, they moved production out of Cincinnati. In 2006, brothers Christopher and Patrick Rose brought Rookwood Pottery back to Cincinnati. Martin and Marilyn Scripps Wade invested in the company, eventually taking it over from 2010 to 2015.[38]

Today, Rookwood is back in production on Race Street in Over-the-Rhine. For more information on Rookwood Pottery and products, visit www.Rookwood.com.

For many decades, the original Rookwood Pottery facility in Mount Adams intermittently served as the Rookwood restaurant, with the great brick kilns as the focal point. In a few iterations, diners could be seated in the kilns for their meals. (It was a great setting for diners who had hearing difficulties.) The last version of the restaurant closed in 2016. As of this writing, none other has taken its place.

PUBLIC LIBRARY OF CINCINNATI AND HAMILTON COUNTY

Once upon a time, historical novelist James Alexander Thom was on faculty at a writers' workshop in Indiana. The discussion concerned the value of computers and the Internet. He turned to one participant who lived in Cincinnati and said, "With a library like Cincinnati's public library downtown, what could you possibly need the Internet for?"

Well, except that the Public Library of Cincinnati and Hamilton County is not open at three o'clock in the morning, he had a good point.

The main branch of the Public Library of Cincinnati and Hamilton County originally occupied a building on Vine Street that was built in 1874. (Many of the rare books in the library are originals from its collection.) It had been designed by John W. McLaughlin, who also designed the Shillito building. On January 27, 1955, the old library was closed. Four days later, the library reopened in its new facility at Eighth and Vine Streets, designed by architect Woodie Garber.

It seems a shame to refer to it as "the library," because it is composed of forty-one branches throughout Cincinnati's fifty-two neighborhoods. These branches are friends in the neighborhood with computers, Internet access, story hours, free public programs and more. The library has received a five-star rating for multiple consecutive years from *Library Journal*, based on usage and circulation. Not only that, but the library is a good community citizen, receiving an award for recycling innovation from the Hamilton County Recycling and Solid Waste District. The awards from the county were even produced with the library's MakerSpace laser engraver. These exciting book production facilities are found not just at the main branch downtown but also in branches in St. Bernard and Reading. MakerSpace allows library customers to design and print their own books, with such amenities as 3D printers, a laser printer, vinyl cutters, sewing machines and an audio recording booth.[39]

According to the 2015 annual report, the library is experiencing record-breaking usage: 18.7 million items borrowed and 3.1 million items downloaded or streamed. With such statistics, the library ranks fifth nationally. In Hamilton County, 80 percent of households have at least one family member with a

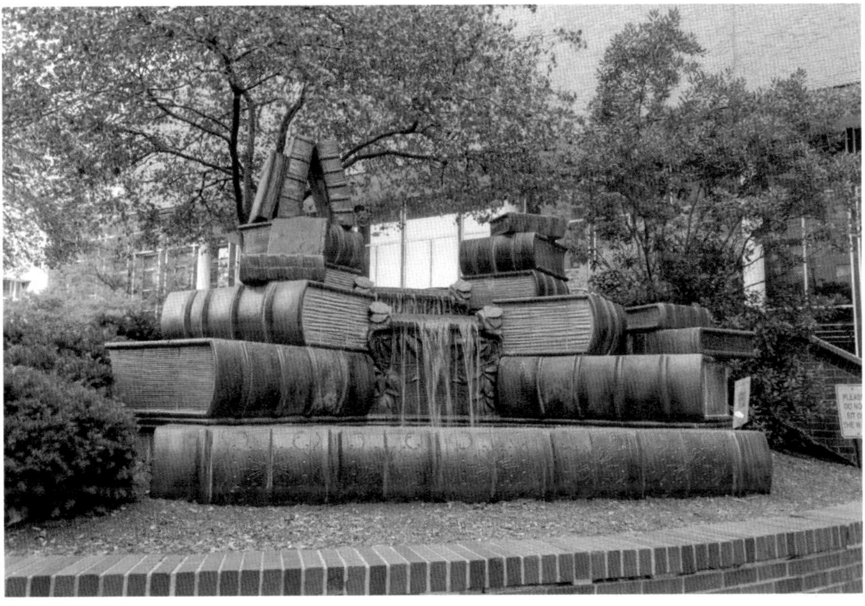

The Amelia Valerio Weinberg Memorial Fountain at the Public Library of Cincinnati and Hamilton County. *Carol M. Highsmith, Library of Congress.*

library card. (Library cards can also be issued to residents of Kentucky's Campbell, Kenton and Boone Counties.)

The library has also added new services, such as MyLibrarian and Book HookUp, to better serve its customers. With the former, patrons can call or ask online for sources and get answers within a day or two. With the latter, customers can fill out a short survey identifying their tastes and interests and, in return, receive reading suggestions from the librarians. Of course, for quick questions, Ask a Librarian is just a phone call (513-369-6900), text (66746) or e-mail (comments.email@CincinnatiLibrary.org) away. Most branches also offer education and homework support, with free wireless Internet and computer access.

The library is not just about books these days; it is about so much more. But the books are still fantastic.

Everything But The House®

One of the things that's changing in Cincinnati is *how* we do business, including family business. Jacquie Denny, founder and chief development officer at Everything But The House (EBTH), is a history buff with a background in sales and corporate management. She was motivated to change the estate-sales business by a memory from her own past. When a great-aunt died in the mid-1970s, Denny witnessed the anguish and hassle the family had to go through to divest the estate of a lifetime of accumulated items.[40]

"She had a big house full of magnificent stuff, but we were limited to just local buyers," says Denny. "And we knew that the people who bought things would make more money than the family did by selling them."

Denny knew there had to be a better business model, so with a partner she founded Sorting It Out. Through it, they applied a project management approach to estate sales. Denny notes that the task of selling off a loved one's estate, or even "right-sizing" one's own, can be physically demanding and emotionally exhausting.

"We provided *the* white glove concierge service for fifteen years," Denny says with pride. Then her partner went back to the 9-to-5 world, and Denny found herself wanting to kick the business up a notch.

Enter Brian Graves. He worked in IT at Children's Hospital. He had been attending Denny's auctions for ten years while he rehabbed a Victorian home in Pleasant Ridge.

"I know he had the same heart and passion for the family that I did," says Denny. "He was all about the service aspect."

As "chief learning officer," Graves had the idea to take the business online. Denny was leery at first.

"I said, 'Dude, I can barely use a smart phone!'" she says. But Graves was persuasive and on the right track. They took the business to the interwebs (at www.EBTH.com) and launched EBTH in 2008 as the "premier estate sale marketplace."

The premise is simple. When a family wants to sell items, regardless of the reason, they contact EBTH. Their experts come in for a free consultation and look at what's for sale and what's not. (Anything that is not sold is donated, kept by the owner or discarded.) The items are photographed and posted on the website, starting with a minimum bid of one dollar. (Yes, they even sell the kitchen sink.) Thousands of items are added daily by sellers from twenty-seven markets across the country (as of 2017). Buyers can see

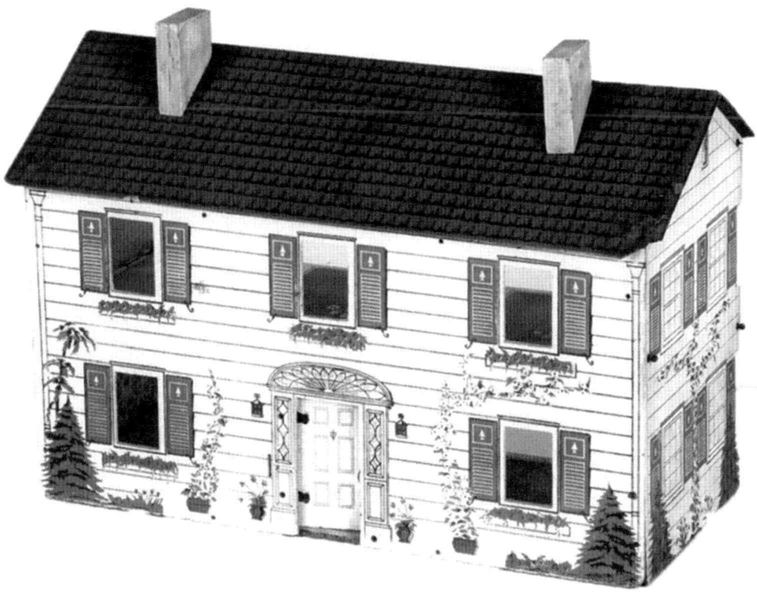

Everything But The House offers a modern approach to estate sales (and sometimes even includes the house, like this vintage dollhouse). *Everything But The House.*

the items from all over the world. No antique auction aficionado could visit that many estate sales in a day in person. From the seller's point of view, the experience is much kinder than having strangers cutting across the grass and handling the merchandise.

"We tell the story about the person," says Denny. "So it becomes a storytelling event and not just people tramping through your front yard." Denny likes to think that they change the estate experience from a dreaded process to one that brings some closure to the family. "Otherwise, you have only five hours to sell a whole lifetime collection and only to the people who can be there in person."

Denny and Graves strive to create a process that is transparent and accessible. EBTH doesn't have a typical client, but they all seem to have thirty or forty years' worth of belongings to get rid of. One group of sisters recently threw a wine and pizza party for themselves while they watched the auction taking place online.

One atypical client was the family of Shirley Mason, who was better known under the pseudonym "Sybil." She was the subject of a book and movie detailing a life that allegedly started out with extreme abuse, which caused what was then called multiple personality disorder (now known as dissociative identity disorder). One of Mason's therapies was painting. The 103 paintings that she created represented the many personalities that she had manifested for her psychiatrist. In recent years, the veracity of this story has been called into question, but the paintings were real. They stayed in the family and finally ended up in a closet. Denny says it wasn't one of the biggest sales, but it was one of the more unusual.

Susan Lucci, once the queen of daytime TV, decided to sell her collection of her clothes and personal belongings, which included *All My Children* keepsakes ranging back several years. The family contacted EBTH.

EBTH has provided services for some of the oldest Cincinnati families and their belongings. Their names can even be found elsewhere in this book—Roebling, Shillito, Procter, Heimlich, Armstrong.

"You know, Neil Armstrong was a very private human being. He never wanted others to profit off his celebrity," Denny says. "One other awesome Cincinnatian whose collection we handled was Dr. Henry Heimlich." Jean-Robert de Cavel favors EBTH when searching for posters for decorating his northern Kentucky home.

In March 2017, the *Cincinnati Business Courier* named EBTH one of the finalists for its Fast 55 Award, representing the fastest-growing private companies in the Greater Cincinnati area that had at least $1 million in

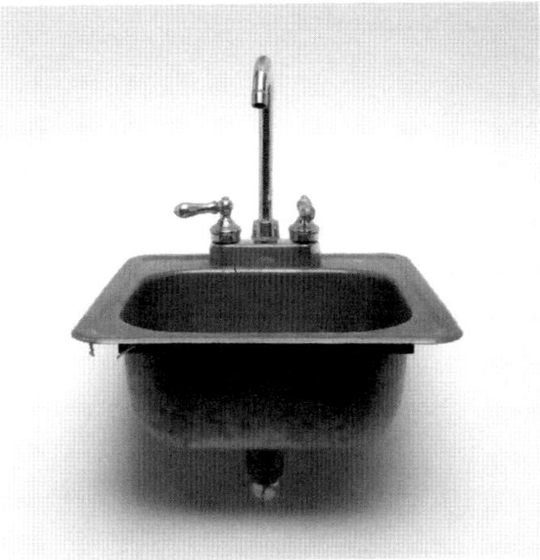

Everything But The House sells everything and the kitchen sink, including this beautiful brass sink. *Everything But The House.*

average revenue over three years. It was also named as a finalist for the *Cincinnati Business Courier*'s 2017 Innovation and Technology Awards.

"We wanted to create a platform that was accessible to everyone from Susan Lucci to the couple next door," says Denny. "We think this platform has changed the way we go through passages in life."

FRAMERI

When Konrad Billetz was eleven years old, he was accidentally shot in the eye by a friend with a BB gun. Doctors feared that he would go blind from the injury, but luckily, this was not the case. However, because of the accident, he has always had to wear corrective lenses. He was distressed that although he could change his clothes with the occasion or mood, he was stuck with one set of glasses. He decided it was time to look at spectacles in a new way. He created Frameri, a company that offers interchangeable lenses in interchangeable frames. It's changing how people buy their glasses and has put Billetz on the *Forbes* 30 Under 30 list in manufacturing and industry.

Frameri has a selection of men's and women's frames, designed here in Cincinnati and offered in its Over-the-Rhine store or online. Customers bring or enter their prescriptions online and select their frames. The website even offers a "virtual try on" so customers can see what they'll look like. With a thirty-day money-back guarantee, customers can rest assured that they will be pleased with the result. Customers can order empty frames to try on at home before ordering the lenses. Any frames they don't like can be returned

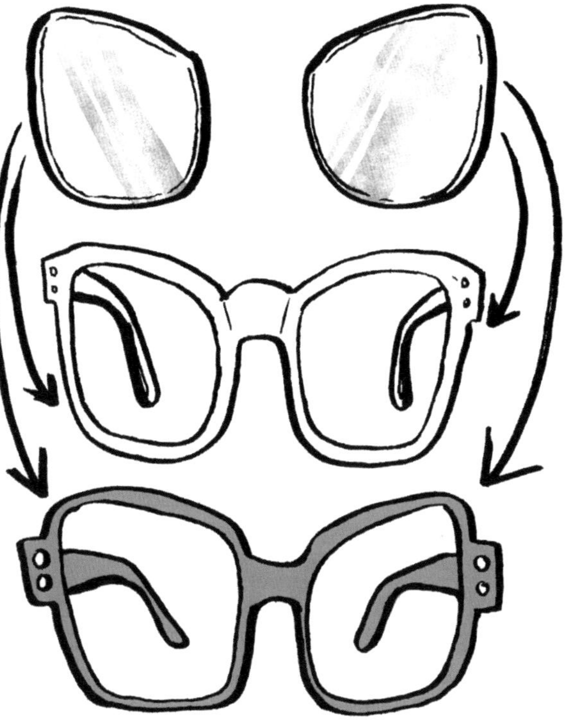

Frameri offers interchangeable lenses and frames to fit any wardrobe or mood. *Illustration by Allison Ranieri.*

within thirty days. Frameri even offers the Terra line of frames for people with big heads.

Prescription lenses start at fifty dollars and can be ordered as single vision, no-line bifocals or sunglasses. The sunglasses even come in three different lens colors. Nonprescription lenses are also available. No other company offers interchangeable frames and lenses from the comfort of the customer's own home.

The average Frameri customer is about twenty-eight years old. Many customers are right here in the Cincinnati area, and they range from businesspeople to stay-at-home moms. One customer even has twelve frames and six sets of lenses![41]

To get started on your frame wardrobe, visit www.frameri.com.

CHAPTER 4
CUSTOMS

Coney Island

Transplants from the East Coast might be surprised to find Coney Island in Cincinnati. But there it is, right off Kellogg Avenue, gracing the banks of the Ohio River.

The land on which Coney Island sits was originally an apple orchard. James Parker, the owner of the farm, encouraged people to come all the way from Cincinnati to have picnics, play games and enjoy the outdoors there. It became known as "Ohio Grove, the Coney Island of the West," when Parker sold the park to the Ohio Grove Corporation in 1886. The next year, the "Ohio Grove" was dropped.

Cincinnatians arrived by the boatload—literally. The first *Island Queen*, a side-wheeler steamboat built in 1896 at a cost of $80,000, could take as many as three thousand passengers from downtown to Coney Island. Sadly, the first *Island Queen* burned when a boat moored next to it caught fire. A second *Island Queen* was then built in 1925 at almost five times the cost of the original. It ran until 1947, when, tragically, it was also destroyed by fire. (A spark from a welder's torch caused the oil tanks to explode. Nineteen crew members were killed.)[42]

Enjoying Coney Island became a tradition for many Cincinnatians—but not all. In 1952, future Cincinnati Council member and vice-mayor Marian Spencer was told by a Coney Island employee that she could

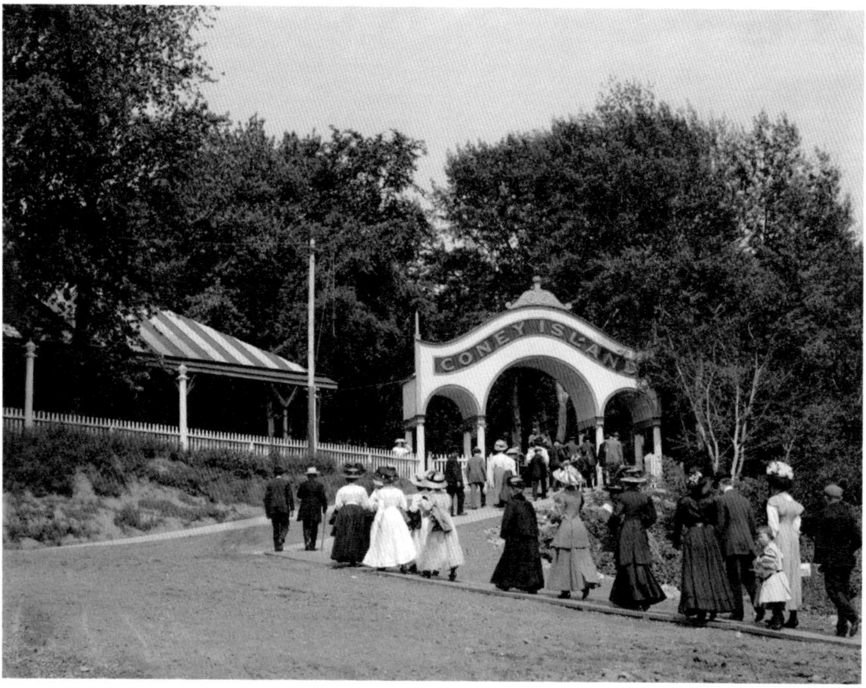

Cincinnati's Coney Island Amusement Park started in the 1870s as Parker's Grove, a former apple orchard. *Library of Congress.*

not bring her children to the park because she was African American. With other Cincinnati leaders, Spencer sued Coney Island to open its doors to African Americans. Not until the city announced, in 1955, that it might not renew Coney Island's license if it did not allow in African Americans did the park open its doors. But not its diving board. Sunlite Pool—the largest recirculating swimming pool in North America—was still restricted to whites only. Finally, in May 1961, Sunlite Pool was also open to people of all colors, races and creeds. Sunlite Pool is now known as Sunlite Water Adventure, complete with slides and other features. Sunlite Pool holds three million gallons of water and takes about three days to fill.[43]

Part of Coney's charm has always been its proximity to the Ohio River. Unfortunately, that proximity also presents the problem of frequent floods. In the late '60s, park owners began talking to Taft Broadcasting Company about shoring up the park to make it more flood resistant. Taft Broadcasting ended up buying Coney Island. However, instead of "waterproofing" the

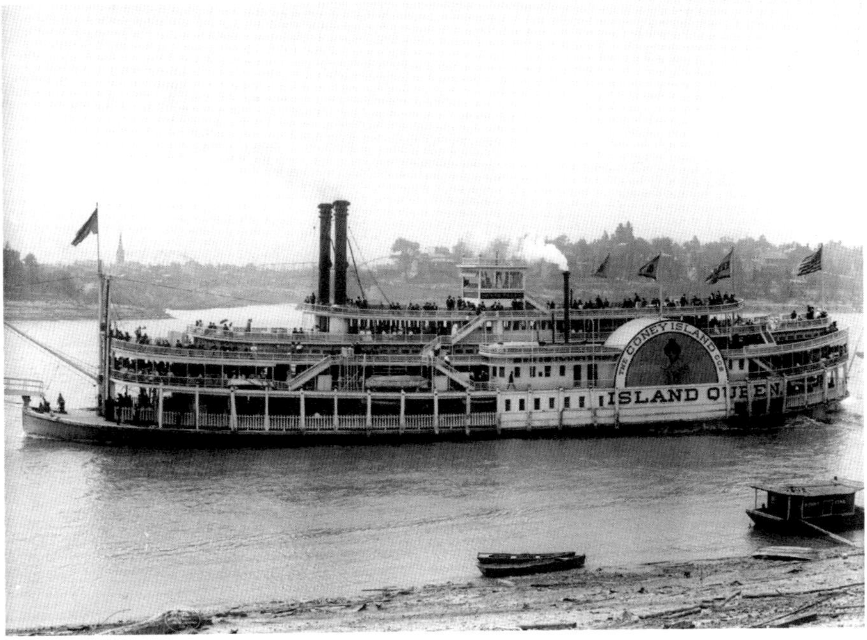

The *Island Queen* en route to Coney Island. Detroit Publishing Co., 1906. *Library of Congress.*

park, it decided to rebuild—in Warren County, as Kings Island. Most of Coney's rides were moved north to Kings Island, and Coney closed its amusement area in 1971. The park reopened in 1973 as a smaller version of its former self.[44]

Coney has many of the attractions of an old-style amusement park, as well as more modern entertainment. One such facility is Moonlight Pavilion. It was originally constructed as an open-air dance hall called Moonlight Dansant (which means moonlight dancing) but quickly became known as Moonlight Gardens. Eventually, it was covered and reinforced with a floor that would survive floods better. It is now called Moonlight Pavilion and is a favorite venue for concerts and wedding receptions.

One of the other attractions that people associate with Coney Island is Riverbend Music Center, although they are not affiliated with each other. Designed by renowned architect Michael Graves, Riverbend opened in 1984 and hosts performers from all over the country. It is also the summer home of the Cincinnati Symphony and Pops Orchestra. Riverbend sits on fifteen acres of former Coney property where two rides used to be.

Besides being a great place for fun and entertainment, Coney Island also hosts a number of annual Cincinnati events, such as the Appalachian Festival, the Summerfair Arts Festival, the Cincinnati Celtic World Festival and the Cincinnati Flower and Farm Fest. For more information, go to coneyislandpark.com.

Riverfest

Cincinnati says *sayonara* to summer every year with a bang. The Western & Southern/WEBN Fireworks presented by Cincinnati Bell at Riverfest is a spectacular extravaganza of music and fireworks, right over the Ohio River. Spectators line both the north and south banks of the Ohio to watch the thirty-minute display. The fireworks are provided by Rozzi Famous Fireworks, which has been in business since 1895. Many people also arrive by boat and fill the river. The best place to be is, of course, there in person, but other venues are suitable for those with sensitive ears. Many of the restaurants and businesses in both Cincinnati and northern Kentucky offer special Riverfest packages, whereby you can view the fireworks and have a snack at the same time. These opportunities fill up fast. Riverfest is also shown on one of the local television stations, often with a simulcast radio broadcast.

Riverfest is held every year at Sawyer Point over Labor Day weekend. In 2017, the festivities start at noon on September 3 and celebrate forty years of Riverfest. Thanks to changes over the years, the Sawyer Point activities are very family friendly, with no alcohol or smoking permitted.

Oktoberfest

Oktoberfest Zinzinnati is the second largest in the world, behind only Munich's. Since 1976, Cincinnatians and their *freunde* have gathered for three days in mid-September to drink beer, eat wursts and do the Chicken Dance. In 1994, Cincinnati set a Guinness record for the most people simultaneously doing the Chicken Dance: forty-eight thousand. Each year, a celebrity takes the stage to lead the dancing. Vendors in booths line the street to sell food, soft drinks and beer—all with a German theme. At either end of the stretch, music and dancing can be found on the Christian Moerlein stages.

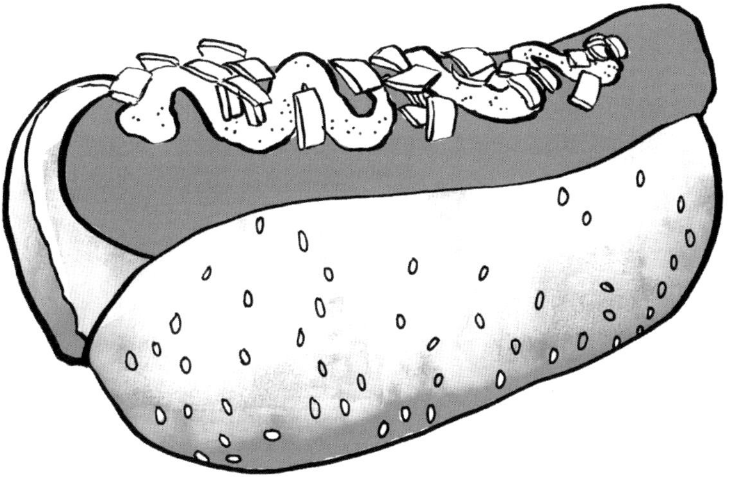

Oktoberfest Zinzinnati is the second-largest Oktoberfest in the world. *Illustration by Allison Ranieri.*

Every year, the event is kicked off in true Midwest fashion with the "Running of the Wieners": a race of about one hundred dachshunds. Each year, one dachshund is named King (or Queen, I hope) of the Wiener Dogs. Another crowd favorite is the Gemütlichkeit [Goodwill] Games, which take place on Friday night. Not to be missed are the Beer Stein Race and Beer Barrel Roll.

If you come, wear comfortable shoes for walking, strolling and dancing. Bring your appetite, too: you'll be stuffed like a sausage by the time you leave. In fact, the half million people who attended Oktoberfest in 2015 consumed the following:

- 87,542 mettwursts
- 80,500 bratwursts
- 64,000 sauerkraut balls
- 56,250 sausages
- 24,640 potato pancakes
- 23,004 soft pretzels
- 20,000 cream puffs
- 16,002 strudels
- 6,000 jumbo pickles
- 3,600 pounds of sauerkraut
- 1,875 pounds of German potato salad
- 702 pounds of Limburger cheese
- 700 pigtails
- 400 pickled pigs' feet[45]

Flying Pig Marathon

People in Cincinnati love to eat. Luckily, they love to run, too. Every year on the first weekend of May, the Flying Pig Marathon hosts more than 36,000 runners and walkers, along with approximately 100,000 "Street Squealers" lining the course. The 2018 race will be the Pig's twentieth anniversary. The Pig offers 5K, 10K, "Flying Fur," open relay, half marathon, full marathon and a few other events. The Pig is one of the certified courses that qualifies runners for the Boston Marathon. Each year about 200 participants in the Pig make it to Massachusetts.[46]

Since its first marathon in 1999, the Pig has grown every year. In addition to the thousands of competitors and spectators, the Flying Pig relies on the hard work of about six thousand "grunts" who work the event. The Flying Pig entertains even those who don't like to run.

Through both the runners and the grunts, a lot of money is raised for charity. The runners encourage their families and friends to sponsor them. The grunts work in exchange for a donation to the charity of their choice. It can hardly be called "work," though. Although it is definitely

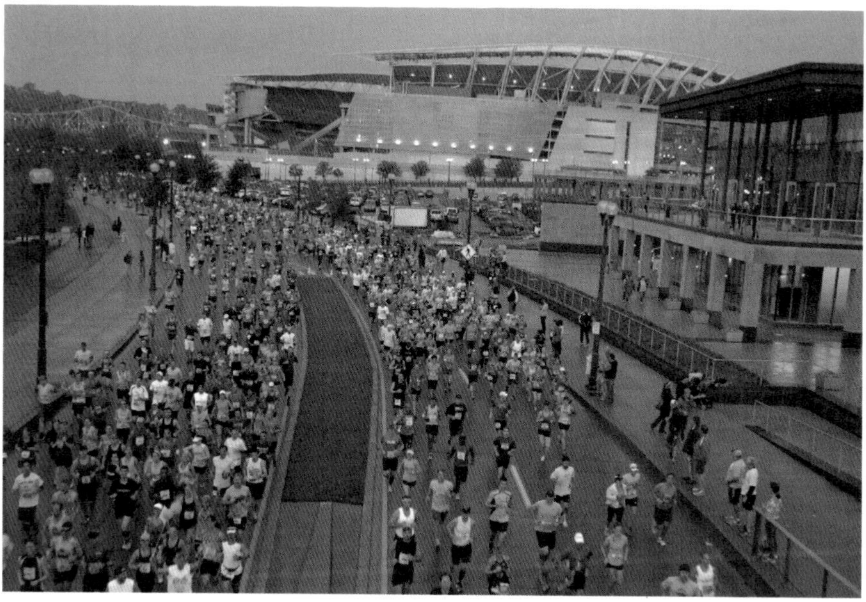

The Flying Pig Marathon, held the first weekend in May, attracts more than thirty-five thousand runners and walkers, with about six thousand "grunts"—volunteers who make the race an annual success. *Michael E. Anderson/Flying Pig Marathon.*

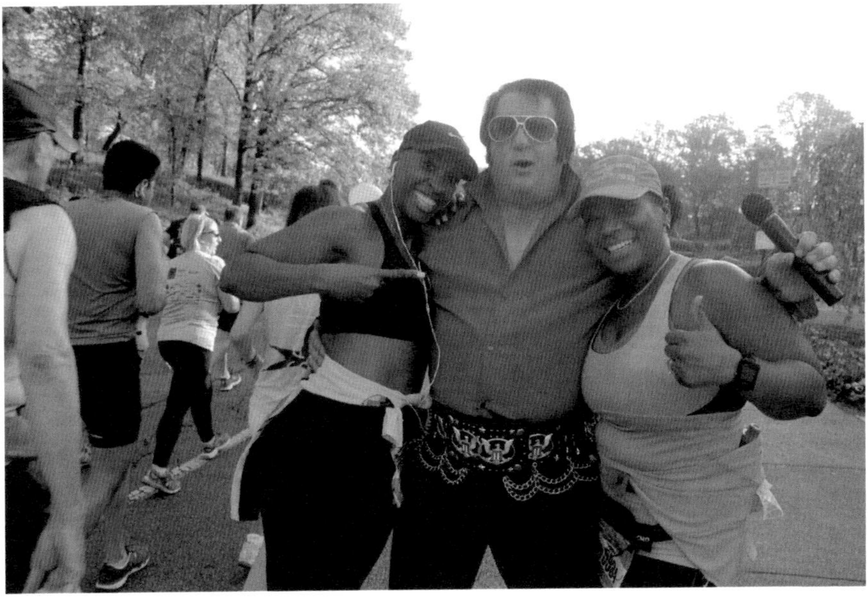

Elvis shows that the Flying Pig Marathon is not just for runners. *Michael E. Anderson/Flying Pig Marathon.*

a workout, volunteering for the Pig is truly a labor of love. In the almost twenty years of "Flying Piganthropy," more than $14 million has been raised for charities. Learn how to be a grunt or sign up for next year's race at flyingpigmarathon.com.

TASTE OF CINCINNATI

Taste of Cincinnati is the longest-running culinary arts festival in the country, starting in 1979 in Piatt Park (then called Garfield Park). The festival was the brainchild of Frisch's Karen Maier, vice president of marketing. She wanted to emulate New York City's Taste of the Big Apple. In its first year, about five thousand people attended the one-day event, where they sampled local restaurants' offerings at appetizer prices. By 1981, the event had expanded to two days, still held over Memorial Day weekend. In 1988, the venue moved to Central Parkway to accommodate the increasing crowds, with a third day and entertainment provided. After Fountain Square was renovated, the festival moved in 2007 to Fifth Street,

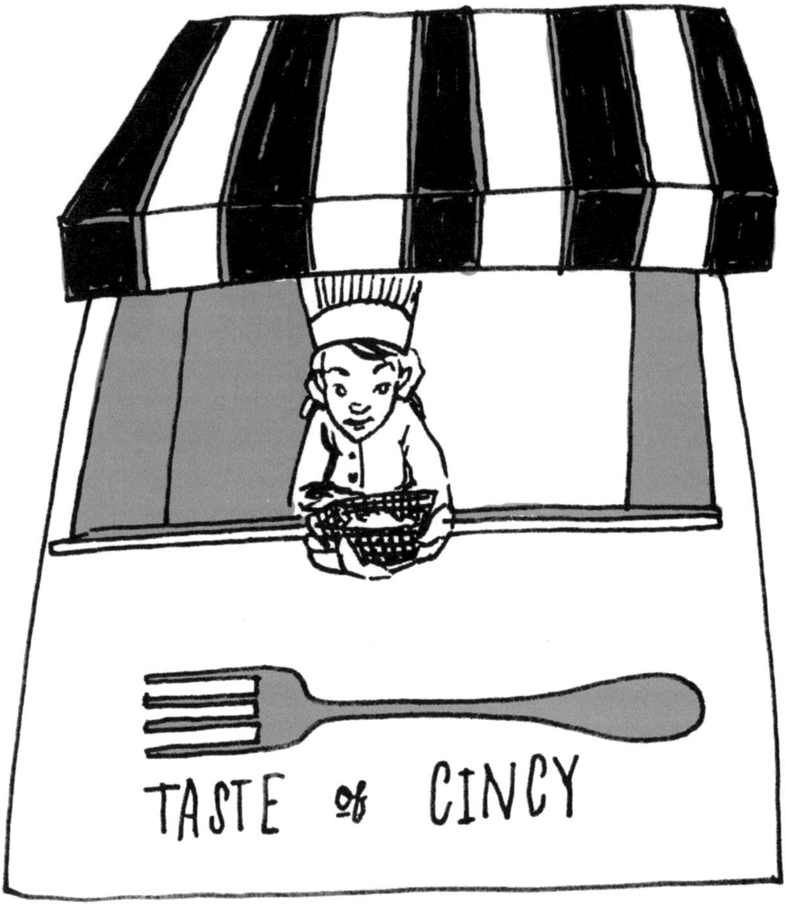

Taste of Cincinnati is an annual food fest that takes place on Memorial Day weekend. *Illustration by Allison Ranieri.*

in the heart of downtown Cincinnati. In 2017, the affair was moved a couple of blocks east to accommodate the new streetcar.

Now, approximately half a million people attend the three-day event, where more than forty restaurants and breweries offer 300 menu items and 102 types of beer. In recent years, some booths have focused on providing vegan and healthy options. Visit www.tasteofcincinnati.com for more information.

FESTIVAL OF LIGHTS

One of the coolest adventures in Cincinnati can be found in the middle of winter at the Cincinnati Zoo and Botanical Garden: the PNC Festival of Lights. Currently in its thirty-fifth year, the Festival of Lights transforms the familiar grounds of the zoo into a sparkly winterland for diverse kids of all ages.

Using 2.5 million LED lights, the zoo personnel highlight the zoo's flora and fauna displays. Besides viewing the zoo under the cover of night, visitors can also take advantage of special activities: a black light puppet show by Madcap Puppets, a train ride courtesy of the BB&T Toyland Express, a gingerbread village, a scavenger hunt, a magical fairy land and much more. One of the most stunning displays is the "Wild Lights" on the zoo's Swan Lake. Top off the visit with snacks and a visit with Santa.[47]

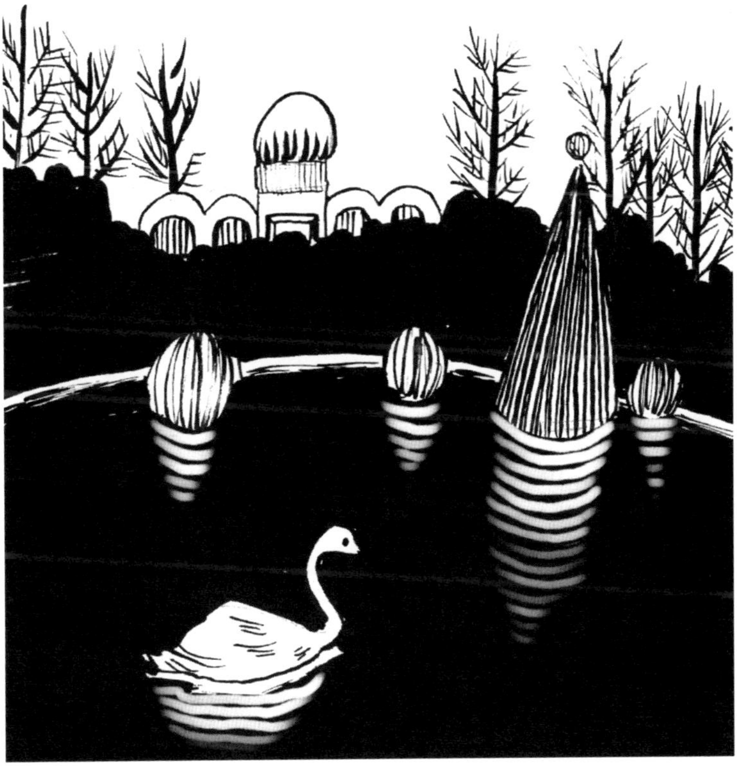

The Festival of Lights is held at the Cincinnati Zoo every winter. *Illustration by Allison Ranieri.*

Kings Island

Kings Island's roots are in one of Cincinnati's oldest attractions: Coney Island. In 1968, the Wachs family (who owned Coney) started exploring the idea of moving Coney Island to get away from the Ohio River, which often flooded, and to put more distance between it and a park that was possibly going to be put in Kentucky. They sold the park to Taft Broadcasting in July of the following year. Taft Broadcasting bought 1,600 acres in Warren County with the intention of moving Coney Island's rides to the new site. The new park was called Kings Island because it was in Kings Mills and it came from Coney Island.

By the end of 1971, the rides from Coney had been installed: Dodgem, Scrambler, Log Flume, Tumblebug and others. They were installed in a part of the park called Coney Mall. Meanwhile, the Eiffel Tower—Kings Island's biggest landmark—was completed at the same time. Finally, after two years of construction, Kings Island opened to the public in 1972.

About that time, Hollywood came to Kings Island. *The Partridge Family* and *The Brady Bunch*, two very popular shows, filmed episodes in the park. Soon after that, Karl Wallenda, famous aerialist, broke a record on the high wire. Daredevil Evel Knievel successfully completed a motorcycle jump over fourteen Greyhound buses in the parking lot.

Kings Island has achieved worldwide recognition for its groundbreaking rides. In 1977, the Screamin' Demon became the first steel looping roller coaster in the country. The famous Beast roller coaster opened in 1979; it was marketed as the "Biggest, Baddest, Longest, Fastest" wooden roller coaster in the world. In 1981, Kings Island introduced a new idea in roller coasters. The Bat was a steel roller coaster where the cars were suspended from above. Unfortunately, the computer often shut down the ride because of mechanical problems, so it was dismantled in 1984. The park introduced another concept new to the United States in the King Cobra, the first coaster where the riders stood up. King Cobra ran through 2001. In 1987, the park introduced Vortex, a steel roller coaster that turned riders upside-down six times—more times than any other such ride in the world. Although Kings Island had water rides, such as the log flumes, it entered a new world with its WaterWorks addition to the park. In 2000, Son of Beast was introduced as the world's tallest, fastest and only looping roller coaster made of wood.

Kings Island's innovations continued not just in its rides but in its seasons. It became the first park in the country to open in the winter of 1982. Winterfest was a great success. The park has opened for Halloween under the name of FearFest, then Howl-O-Fest, then Trick-or-Treat with Dinosaurs.

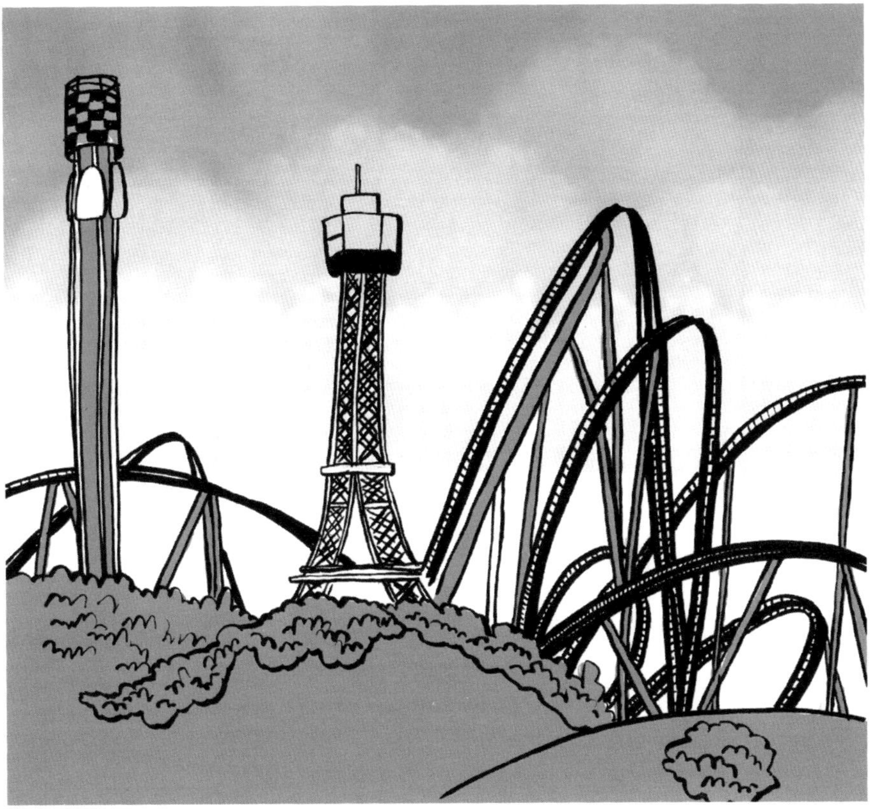

Since 1972, Kings Island has been thrilling visitors, including the *Partridge Family* and the *Brady Bunch*. *Illustration by Allison Ranieri.*

In 1992, Paramount purchased the Kings Entertainment Company, thus making the park Paramount's Kings Island. Some of the rides and attractions that had Hanna-Barbera themes began migrating to Nickelodeon themes and characters. In 2001, Hanna-Barbera Land was renamed Nickelodeon Central; in 2006, it became Nickelodeon Universe.[48]

Kings Island was sold in 2006 to Cedar Fair (which then owned the three largest amusement parks in Ohio). It is still a force to be reckoned with, with its eighty rides, fifteen roller coasters, thirty-three-acre water park and many live shows and attractions. (However, the Kings Island live African animal exhibit closed.) In 2015, Kings Island was the second-most visited seasonal amusement park in the United States (behind fellow Ohio park Cedar Point) and was third overall in North America, with about 3.2 million visitors annually.[49]

Chapter 5
Food

Chili

Cincinnati chili is different from most other chilis: no hot jalapeño or habanero peppers, no chunks of stew beef, no colorful flashes of diced bell peppers. Instead, the palate tastes nuances of allspice, garlic and cumin. Some people swear they taste cinnamon, cocoa and Worcestershire sauce. Cincinnati chili is also not served in a bowl with a piece of corn bread on the side but on spaghetti, accompanied by a bag of oyster crackers.

Many people point out that Cincinnati's chili is Greek, and that's why it's different. But that's not completely correct. Cincinnati's first chili makers were brothers Tom and John Kiradjieff, who emigrated from what we now know as the Republic of Macedonia (just north of Greece) and ended up in Cincinnati.

In 1922, the Kiradjieffs opened a hot dog shop in the burlesque theater on Vine Street between Eighth and Ninth Streets. It had been called the Gaiety Theatre, but now it was called the Empress. The Kiradjieffs planned to serve Greek food in addition to the hot dogs, but their home cooking was not finding a wide audience. To broaden their appeal to their very German clientele, they concocted a recipe that was reminiscent of the flavors of their homeland and then doctored it.

"They added a dozen spices like chili, plus garlic and onions, and ground beef," Tom's son Joe said in an October 2013 interview. He described how his father and uncle came up with their unique recipe, but he still hedged when describing the spices, even after more than ninety years of the family business.

The brothers served the mixture steaming hot over spaghetti. It was a big hit. They called their restaurant Empress Chili, after the burlesque theater. When his father's health declined, Joe Kiradjieff started operating the Empress empire in the 1950s. Joe retired in 2009, after selling Empress to another chili family.

If you go to Greece, you might find stews with the flavors that resemble Cincinnati's chili but nothing called "chili" with cheese on the top and spaghetti on the bottom. You certainly won't find any three-way, four-way or five-ways; the Kiradjieffs came up with that concept. A three-way is spaghetti, chili and cheese. A four-way adds beans or onions. A five-way adds both. They served a plate with a couple of hot dogs on the side with some steaming chili and cheese on top (known as "Coneys" after New York's Coney Island).

In the 1920s, a young Greek named Nicholas Sarakatsannis stopped in the Empress Chili parlor looking for a job and was immediately put to work. Within short order, he felt he could come up with a better recipe but didn't want to compete directly with the Kiradjieffs, so he crossed the river. Thus, in 1928, Dixie Chili was born in Newport, where it still operates today just north of Eighth Street. It has since expanded in many ways. It has three locations, many food offerings and even a six-way, composed of chili, spaghetti, beans, onions, cheese and fresh garlic.

Another Greek Nicholas got his start with the Kiradjieffs: Nicholas Lambrinides. Like Nicholas Sarakatsannis, Lambrinides wanted to open his own chili parlor, so he headed for Price Hill. In 1949, he and three of his sons opened the first Skyline Chili parlor at the intersection of Glenway and Quebec Avenues. The original westside parlor has been demolished, but Skylines can be found throughout Cincinnati and as far away as Naples, Florida.

In 1940, a single chili parlor quietly opened in Camp Washington, logically called Camp Washington Chili. In 1951, Johnny Johnson—then a Greek immigrant, now the Johnson family patriarch—started working at Camp Washington Chili, and he's never worked anywhere else. Although the restaurant was rebuilt because of widening of the street, it has always been right where it is now: Hopple Street off I-75.

Camp Washington Chili was featured on Travel Channel's *Man vs. Food* and has won numerous awards, including a James Beard award in

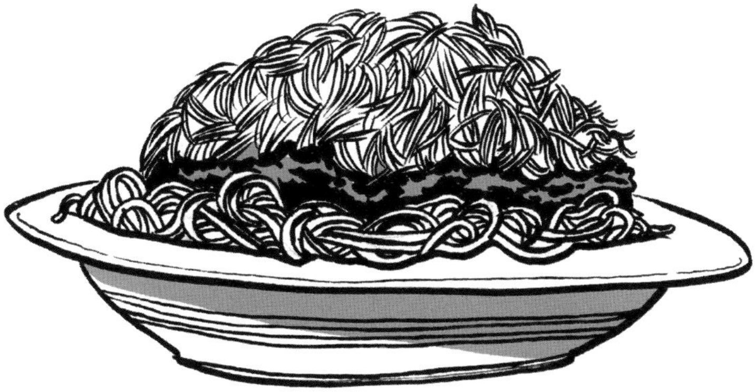

Cincinnati chili is unlike any other chili and is a hotly contested subject in Cincinnati. *Illustration by Allison Ranieri.*

2000. In 2013, *Smithsonian Magazine* named it one of "20 Most Iconic Food Destinations Across America." It was Johnny Johnson's son-in-law, Joe Papakirk, who bought Empress Chili from Joe Kiradjieff in 2009.

Cincinnati boasts about two hundred chili parlors, but the biggest contenders for Greater Cincinnati's favorite chili boil down to Empress, Skyline, Dixie, Camp Washington and Gold Star (started by four Jordanian brothers named Daoud). The best Cincinnati chili is a big debate that will never be settled. One thing that most native Cincinnatians agree on, however, is that chili spaghetti should not be twirled; cut into it so that all the layers are in each bite.[50]

ICE CREAM AND CANDY

Because of Cincinnati's many German and Greek immigrants, the city has had a long tradition of great restaurants. Cincinnati is famous for its "chili wars." But a frosty war wages at the other end of the meal in a bitter battle for the title of best sweets of the Queen City.

However, Graeter's and Aglamesis Brothers are not the only sweet temptations in town. Cincinnati is home to a host of confectionary families. Here's the scoop on four of them, from the oldest to the youngest.

Graeter's

The Graeter family came to the United States in the mid-1880s from Bavaria. Young Louis Charles "Charlie" Graeter worked as a teenager in a market on Court Street, at the foot of the Sycamore hill. One of his assignments was to make ice cream. Because of a lack of refrigeration, he had to make it in small batches using rock salt and ice around the tub of cream and sugar to freeze it into ice cream. This knowledge served him well after he married Regina Berger, and they opened a store of their own. Charlie and Regina established the first Graeter's store in 1870 in East Walnut Hills, at 967 East McMillan. There they made ice cream and candies in the back of the store, sold them in the front and lived upstairs.

After her husband's life was cut short by a streetcar accident in 1919, Regina continued to run the store and created the phenomenal success it is now. She opened a second store in Hyde Park, which is the oldest Graeter's store still operating today.

In 1934, Regina bought a location on Reading Road for expanded production capability. From there, the business is run by Charlie and Regina's great-grandsons: Richard, Bob and (wait for it) Chip. A fourth generation of Graeters runs the company now, with stores as far away as Columbus and Lexington. Still, the dense, delicious ice cream is made the same way that Regina and Charlie made it—two gallons at a time.[51]

Graeter's also offers candies and a full-service bakery. Stop in some morning in any of the twenty Cincinnati shops for a cup of coffee and a kruller. If you're on the road, you can find Graeter's in Chicago, Dayton, Pittsburgh, Cleveland, Indianapolis, Lexington and Louisville. To ship some chips to your friends, go to www.graeters.com.

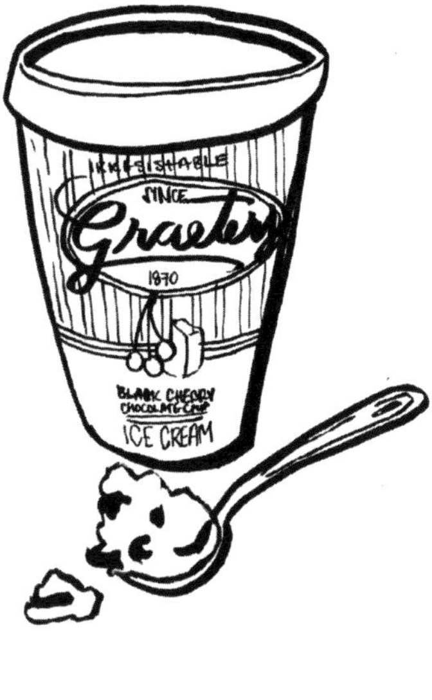

Cincinnati is blessed with many great ice cream makers. Graeter's has been treating Cincinnatians to ice cream since 1870. *Illustration by Allison Ranieri.*

Aglamesis Brothers

In 1908, sixteen-year-old Thomas Aglamesis (pronounced "a-glah-MEE-siss," *not* "a-gluh-MEE-seez") left Sparta, Greece, and his many siblings to seek his fortune in the United States. His father had just died, and as the eldest son, he needed to ensure the welfare of his family. His brother Nicholas soon joined him. They started working in downtown Cincinnati in the "Old Arcade," where they learned how to make ice cream.

They saved up enough to open their own place, and in 1908, they bought a store in Norwood, calling it the Metropolitan. The Aglamesis brothers also churned all their ice cream flavors by hand, using metal cylinders with rock salt and ice to freeze the cream mixture. They soon added candies to their offerings in the store.

In 1913, the Aglamesis brothers bought another store in Oakley, on Madison Avenue, where they made chocolate candy from scratch in the back of the store. This store is the main store today and is a beauty to behold, with Tiffany lamps and marble counters and tabletops from Portugal. In 1922, an ice cream plant was added behind the store to expand production. Gleaming French kettles of copper sit in the plant in which the ice cream is made.[52]

One of the other "offerings" at the Metropolitan was more in the line of "eye candy." The Chakiris family moved from Greece to the United States in 1916. Against patriarch Aristotle's wishes, son Stylianos "Steve" wanted to be an actor. However, Aristotle won, so Steve stayed in the family's confectionary business. He went to work for the Aglamesis brothers at the Metropolitan before going off on his own. In 1933, Steve's son George was born. Seven years later, the family moved to California. There, George was able to achieve his father's dream: he became an actor. He won the 1961 Academy Award for best actor in a supporting role for his role as Bernardo in *West Side Story*.[53]

Caught in the Great Depression, Thomas and Nicholas sold the Metropolitan and changed the name of their company to Aglamesis Brothers. In the 1950s, Nicholas died and Thomas's health was failing, so Thomas's son James took over the company. Jim Aglamesis still runs the company as of this writing. A store has been added, in Montgomery. The chocolate candies and ice cream are still made in the Oakley store, the "sincere" way.

To order some sweets for your sweetheart (or yourself), visit www.aglamesis.com.

Esther Price Candies

Wasn't Esther Price from Dayton? Yes, she was. But many people in Cincinnati think she was a Cincinnatian, and the company that she founded in Dayton is now being run by a second generation of Cincinnatians, so it's worth a nod here.

In a home ec class in school, she learned how to make fudge, and her life was changed forever. Even when she graduated from school and got a job in retail, Esther continued to make candies for her friends and co-workers, to great accolades.

Finally, she gave in to her destiny and opened her own store in 1926. She prided herself on using the finest butter and cream for her candies. She created a local favorite when she and the folks from Mike-Sells (now Mikesells) potato chips teamed up and created the (now famous) chocolate-covered potato chip, available from October to March.

In 1976, Price sold the company to four men from Cincinnati, including one named Jim Day. Today, Jim Day's descendants own Esther Price Candies. Although the company headquarters is still in Dayton, the distinctive gold box can be found in dedicated Esther Price stores in Cincinnati, as well as in many area Kroger supermarkets. Esther Price (born in 1905) died in 1994.[54]

Fawn Candy Company

When Paul "Pep" Guenther returned from World War II in 1946, he and his wife, Jean, opened a candy store in Cheviot. Jean's Greek heritage helped shape the flavors that went into the sweets they created.

Since 1984, Fawn Candy has been owned by Jean and Pep's daughters: Kathy, Jackie, Jean and Jane. They own two stores, one on Harrison Avenue in Green Township and one in Rookwood Pavilion. They've now been joined by their children, nieces, nephews and grandchildren, making four generations of Fawn Candy.[55] They are also great community citizens and often help with local fundraisers through sale of their products. Find them online at www.fawncandy.com.

JEAN-ROBERT DE CAVEL

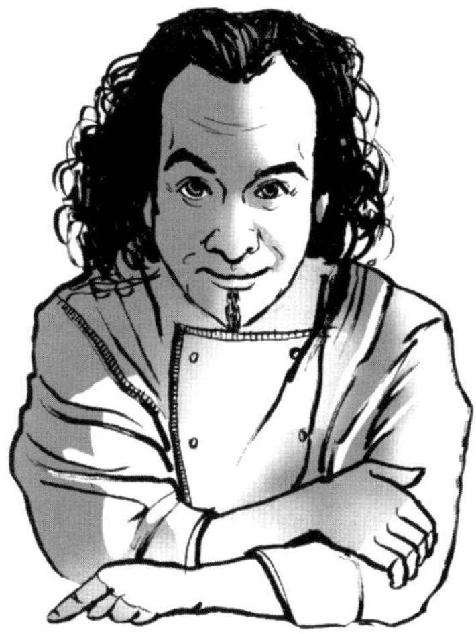

Jean-Robert de Cavel arrived in the early 1990s. Cincinnati cuisine has never been the same since. *Illustration by Allison Ranieri.*

Jean-Robert de Cavel always loved to cook. Even when growing up in Lille, France, he knew his destiny. He told journalist Alyssa Brandt, for a 2013 article in *Cincinnati Magazine*, "Even in the Boy Scouts I wanted to be the cook."[56] De Cavel became an apprentice at a restaurant in a train station while he attended culinary school. After a mandatory military stint, he was off to chase his dream.

In the 1990s, Jean-Robert de Cavel traded in the "bleu, blanc et rouge" of France for the red, white and blue of the USA. As executive chef first at Le Regence (the restaurant for the Plaza Athénée Hotel) and then La Gauloise in New York City, he thought he would stay in the Big Apple. When the owners of La Gauloise started battling, de Cavel was told he could buy them out or leave.

About that time, a friend and fellow chef named Daniel Boulud told de Cavel of the upcoming need for a chef at the Maisonette. Although de Cavel was tempted by the five stars (after all, Le Regence had only four), he was not sure he wanted to move to the Midwest. While his German girlfriend, Annette Pfund—an assistant room service manager at the Plaza Athénée—visited her family in Madrid, de Cavel flew to Cincinnati to cook a meal for the Comisar family, owners of the Maisonette. Because de Cavel's luggage had been lost, he had only his travel clothes for his first night in town. The Maisonette had a very strict dress coat (jacket and tie for men, dresses or skirts for women), so he could not even sample a meal at the Maisonette. Instead, the Comisar cousins, Nat and Marc, took de Cavel to another restaurant of theirs: Chester's Roadhouse in Montgomery.

De Cavel made the short list of three chefs to prepare a meal at the Maisonette. Once the committee tasted his first course, it was a done deal. He, Annette and his cat (Escoffier) moved to Cincinnati, where de Cavel became the *chef de cuisine* at the Maisonette. He thought he might stay three or five years.

The Maisonette was truly one of the gems in the Queen City's crown. De Cavel served as the Maisonette's *chef de cuisine* from 1993 to 2002. For forty-one years, it was ranked as a five-star restaurant by *Mobil Travel Guide*. In fact, it was the most highly ranked restaurant in North America. Nevertheless, it closed its doors in 2005.

De Cavel became the face of Cincinnati cuisine when he entered into a business partnership with Martin and Marilyn Scripps Wade. Through their Jean-Robert French Restaurant Group, they opened several more restaurants. Jean-Robert at Pigall's opened on Fourth Street and earned four Mobil stars. The Jean-Robert French Restaurant Group was also to include the JeanRo Bistro, Pho Paris, Greenup Café, Lavomatic and Twist.[57]

Sadly, as he was getting ready to open the bistro, the de Cavels faced a heartbreaking tragedy when their three-month-old daughter, Tatiana, died from Sudden Infant Death Syndrome. They established the de Cavel Family SIDS Foundation, Eat.Play.Give (www.eatplaygive.net). Through the foundation, they have raised close to $1 million, which has gone to research grants and a memorial scholarship at the Midwest Culinary Institute.

Unfortunately, Wade and de Cavel had a falling out, which ended in closing most of the group's restaurants and de Cavel facing a one-year noncompete agreement. During that year, not able to open any restaurants, de Cavel still stayed busy. He cooked for many charity events, generously giving of his own time and money. He also became the chef-in-residence at Cincinnati State's Midwest Culinary Institute. Thus, instead of (or in addition to) his many "unofficial" protégés, he officially became the mentor for hundreds of would-be chefs.

Currently, the three-time James Beard nominee oversees five restaurants: Jean-Robert's Table (opened in August 2010), French Crust Café (opened in August 2013), Le Bar a Boeuf (opened in March 2015), Restaurant L (opened in August 2016 in partnership with Richard Brown, former maître d'hôtel at the Maisonette) and Frenchie Fresh (opened in September 2016). Learn more about de Cavel at www.jrcincy.com.

FINDLAY MARKET

Established in 1852 and open for business ever since, Findlay Market is the oldest continuous open-air market in Ohio. Reminiscent of European markets, the offerings are fresh, local and often unusual. The story of Findlay Market is unusual, as well.

James Findlay came to Cincinnati with his wife, Jane, in 1793 when the settlement was still called Losantiville. He was among the two dozen people who established the Cincinnati public library in 1802. Findlay served as mayor twice, fought in the War of 1812 and was even taken prisoner by the British. He was elected to Congress, along with his brothers (who represented different districts in Pennsylvania).

Findlay bought a plat of land that was referred to as the Northern Liberties. This section of land was in the wooded area north of Cincinnati. In today's terms, it is described as that area near Elder, Findlay, Elm, Republic, Green, Race and McMicken Streets. He established a market, selling goods that were brought in by horse and mule.

After the death of both Findlays, the property was given to the City of Cincinnati in 1851 to continue as a market. Over the decades, the open

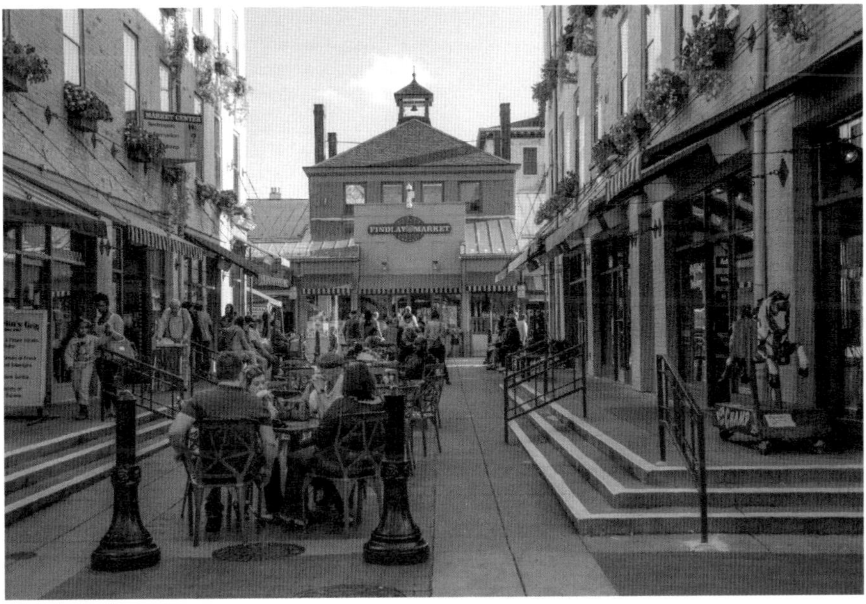

Findlay Market is thought to be the oldest continuous public market in the United States. *Library of Congress.*

market was enclosed, and refrigeration and plumbing were added. It has been upgraded twice, in the 1970s and again in the 2000s.[58]

Currently, merchants sell a variety of goods: artisan gifts, baked goods, beer and wine, catering, cheese and dairy, desserts and chocolate, flowers, seafood, meat and poultry, prepared foods, organic produce, spices and other specialty items.[59]

PRIMAVISTA

Its name translates to "prime view," and it certainly is. It could also be translated as "first sight," as in "love at…," and that would be true, too. Sitting quietly atop Price Hill on Cincinnati's west side, the Primavista restaurant is known equally well for two things: the food and the view. Diners look out upon the Queen City and Ohio River from the west, a view not found many other places. It's a spectacular view day or night. Speaking of night, it is also a popular site for viewing the fireworks of Riverfest, Cincinnati's end-of-summer celebration. But those reservations must be booked months in advance.

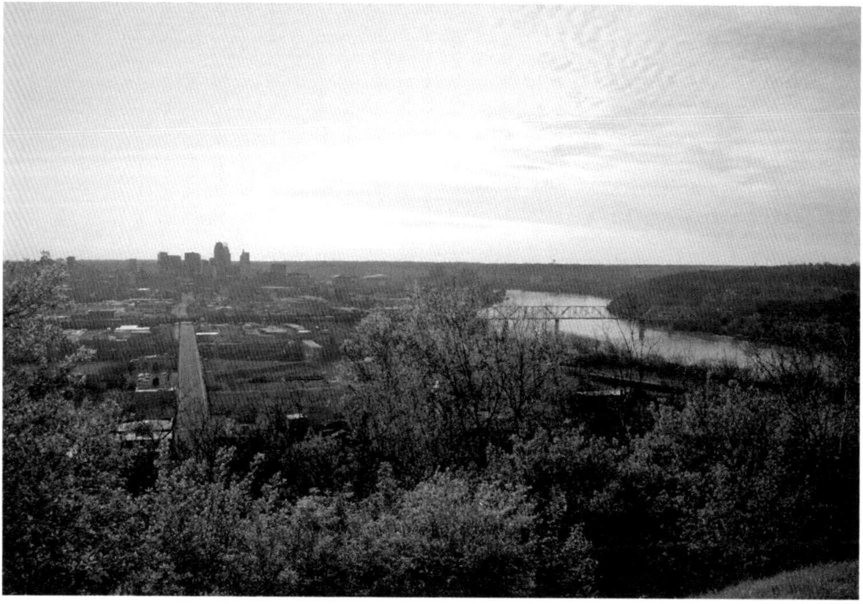

Primavista Restaurant offers a rare view of Cincinnati—from the west side. *Wendy Hart Beckman.*

The dining area is laid out as two tiers so that everyone has a good view of the city. Even without the view, the restaurant is worth a visit—or several—for its scrumptious Italian food. From *carpaccio* to *caffé*, the experience is first rate. A private dining area can be reserved, often popular with wedding parties.

To peruse the menu or make a reservation, go to www.pvista.com.

GREEN BEAN DELIVERY

Subscription-based home delivery of food, such as the currently popular Blue Apron and Hello Fresh, is not a new idea. One could argue that home delivery started with milkmen and their clinking bottles. Even Schwan's Home Service started out as Schwan's Dairy in Minnesota in 1948. Their familiar yellow trucks have brought frozen foods to happy homes for decades. Ever receive holiday packages from Swiss Colony? Hickory Farms? Harry and David? Shari's Berries? Graze? Food delivery services nowadays range from fully prepared meals ready for reheating and ingredients to a full meal with recipe included to desserts or just random snack food.

Now, with advances in refrigeration and packaging, the food delivery service world has exploded. In Cincinnati, bright green-and-white trucks have appeared, bringing to our doorsteps locally grown, fresh foods produced on sustainable farms. Green BEAN Delivery was founded in Indiana in 2007 by spouses Beth Blessing and Matt Ewer. Their goal was to give organic farmers and food artisans a way to reach a broader consumer base. The company quickly grew to "hubs" in Ohio, Kentucky, Missouri and Tennessee. Green BEAN Delivery, Tiny Footprint Distribution, Feel Good Farm (in Indiana) and EcOhio (in Mason, Ohio) make up the BEAN family.

"Our network of growers and artisans is vast. Our greatest asset is our partnerships we've grown throughout the last decade of business," CEO Ewer says. "Right now, we are evolving quickly and our service model is changing. You absolutely have to change to stay relevant in today's food-meets-tech landscape. Our latest and greatest development is our smart phone app. You can now order from us on your phone, and we can connect with our customer in all kinds of cool ways through this platform. It's really changed the way we think about our business and how we design our point of sale platforms."[60]

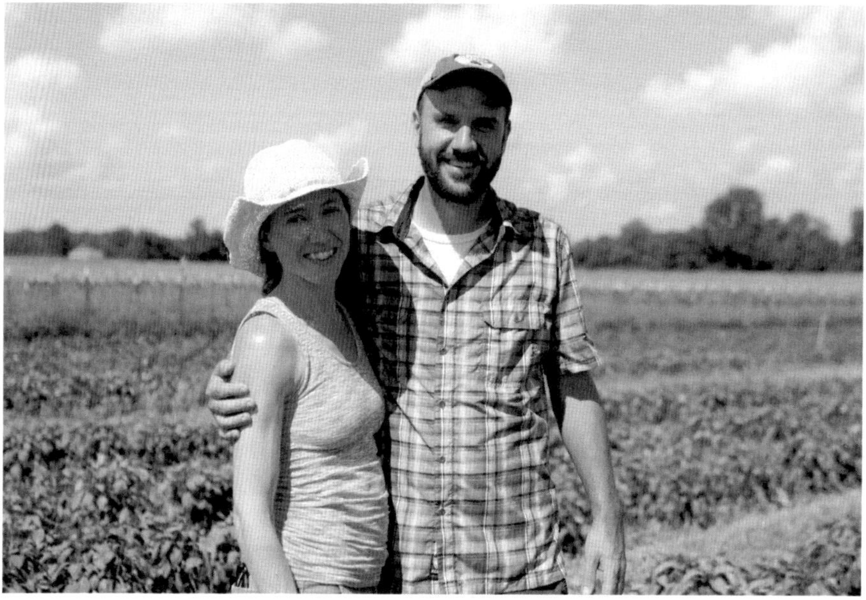

Green BEAN Delivery's founders and husband and wife, Matt Ewer and Beth Blessing. *Green BEAN Delivery.*

Like many modern companies, BEAN also has a philanthropic mission. "I think it's important to understand that we are dedicated to the health of the communities we service," says Ewer. "We provide no unnatural ingredients on our website and focus on sustainable and organic food. We believe our service has a purpose. The BEAN acronym stands for Biodynamic.Education.Agriculture.Nutrition. We have built our business from these cornerstones. In a decade of business, we were able to donate well over one million pounds of fresh produce to local food banks. We are very proud of our efforts to support people in our community that need a helping hand. We thank our customers, our employees and our partners for the opportunity to give back."

BEAN's mission from the start has been "to help mend broken components of our nation's food systems." Whether donating farm-fresh food to the needy or providing personalized food bins to subscribers, BEAN specializes in organic, natural, locally sourced food from hundreds of family farms and artisans.

Subscribers have a choice of ordering different-sized bins and then tailoring them to fit their needs. "Our main consumer is women between thirty and fifty years old with children," says Ewer. "Several 'organically' based companies are driven by mothers. We are certainly no different, as moms are looking to keep their children healthy and have very busy schedules." Ewer says that they are seeing people from a wide variety of income levels who use their service, including several millennials who connect with BEAN on their newly launched smart phone app.

Their most popular items are farm-fresh eggs and dairy. "We have great partnerships in each of the markets we service to provide these products to our customers on a local level," says Ewer.

However, just because they specialize in working with local farms does not mean that customers are constrained to produce from the Midwest. "We recently started selling Young Thai coconuts," Ewer says. "You have to take the top off of the coconut, and then you can enjoy the nutritious water in the core of the coconut. You can also utilize the coconut meat."

Ewer says it goes back to their suppliers. "Just like a chef, if you are going to make a great dish, you have to have really good ingredients," he notes. "My background has always been food. In our scenario, it was food industry professionals doing tech, not tech professionals doing food. That has always been an important aspect of our DNA and one we take pride in. Oh ya, we got some awesome tech too!"

"We've worked very hard to get to where we used to be. The onset of the Internet has been a great tool to get consumers closer to their local farmers and artisans. The future of food is changing and will become less brick and mortar. There will be greater selections for customers and hopefully greater transparency. No matter what the technology [is], the key is always the consumer. Farmers will provide whatever the consumer demands. The avenues to reach the consumer are growing by leaps and bounds each and every day. We are at the tip of the iceberg where food and technology meet. When people ask me what my company does, I let them know we are a tech company that likes to get dirty (we also farm 120 acres of organic vegetables). The truth is we are using technology to help mend a broken food system and provide opportunity and a sustainable pipeline for environmentally friendly producers of good old-fashioned (and sometimes new and innovative) food."

Former Beer Brewing Capital of the United States

Near the Ohio River at the base of Race Street, David Embree opened the first Cincinnati brewery in August 1810. One hundred years later, at the peak of its brewing prowess, Cincinnati had more than thirty breweries supplying about three hundred saloons. Cincinnati was the biggest beer producer outside Europe. The names on today's beer cans and bottles were young men trying to earn a living in a new country back then.

In 1842, at the age of twenty-four, Bavarian Christian Moerlein opened his first business in Cincinnati: blacksmithing. Moerlein sold his blacksmithing business in 1853 and, with a little help from his friends, constructed a brewery on the same site. Less than a year later, he had sold his first beer. Within twelve years, he was able to buy out his partner for $130,000. When Moerlein died in 1897, his assets exceeded $1.5 million—quite an achievement for a man who had arrived in Cincinnati penniless and barely able to speak English. His fellow beer barons Gottlieb Mühlhauser and John Hauck also became millionaires.

Another fine-spirited Cincinnatian of the late 1880s was John Goetz Jr. He married Elisabeth Moerlein, making Christian Moerlein his father-in-law. A lawyer, Goetz became the vice president of Christian Moerlein Brewing Company. He was also very active in the community, sitting on several boards, such as the Cincinnati Board of Fire Commissioners, and serving as the president of the Cincinnati Zoo. He was well liked nationally and locally.

Goetz died suddenly in 1899 from a stroke, just five days short of his forty-fourth birthday (and only two years after Moerlein's death). Despite the deaths of both Moerlein and Goetz, Cincinnati was certainly not at a loss for beer. The Christian Moerlein Brewing Company was still in the capable hands of Christian's son, William.

Louis Hudepohl and George Kotte owned a wholesale liquor business. When Hudepohl Sr. died, his son, Louis Hudepohl II, and Kotte bought the Koehler Brewery (formerly the Buckeye Brewery). Louis II began to buy out his partner. When Kotte died at the age of fifty-six, Hudepohl bought out Kotte's widow, Katharina, but retained the name of the brewery. He changed the name to Hudepohl Brewery after Katharina died.

The United States was moving toward Prohibition, but the Eighteenth Amendment had not been ratified yet. Still, animosity was growing toward those who brewed and consumed alcohol, including beer. The breweries were

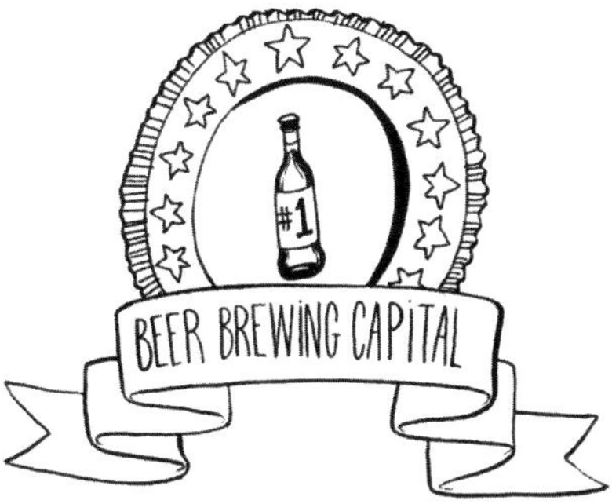

Cincinnati was the mecca of beer brewing in the 1800s. With the many microbreweries popping up, it is celebrating a beer renaissance. *Illustration by Allison Ranieri.*

predominantly owned by Germans, and the United States had just returned from the First World War.

Prohibition—the era during which the manufacture, sale and transportation of intoxicating liquors was outlawed by ratification of the Eighteenth Amendment to the Constitution—began in 1920. For the next thirteen years, Cincinnati was affected, as was the rest of the nation, by this amendment and by the Volstead Act. However, in a way, Cincinnati's loss was worse: by the 1880s, Cincinnati had become the mecca of beer brewing. Virtually all, if not all, of the twenty to thirty breweries were owned by German American or German families. Many Cincinnatians felt that Prohibition took on an anti-German focus. As the axe of Prohibition fell, the last of Cincinnati's breweries to remain were the John Hauck Brewing Company, the Windisch-Mühlhauser Lion Brewery and Christian Moerlein.[61]

Now, in the twenty-first century, Cincinnati is experiencing a brewery renaissance. Christian Moerlein sprang to life in the form of a brewery and restaurant in the Banks entertainment district along the riverfront. CEO Greg Hardman also took over the Hudepohl, Little Kings and Burger labels. Although Sam Adams himself was from Massachusetts and his eponymous brewery calls Boston "home," the major brewery for Sam Adams is right here in Cincinnati. (Some bars are confused about this and list Sam Adams as an import.) Other new breweries include MadTree, Taft's Ale House, Listermann, Bad Tom Smith, Braxton, Rhinegeist, Rivertown, 50West, Urban Artifact and Tap & Screw (in Oakley, in an arrangement with BrewRiver Gastropub). Even Wiedemann's, which was originally founded in 1890 but ceased production in 2006, has had a comeback.

For a tour of the breweries, check out the Cincy Brew Bus (or to enjoy bourbon or wine on their "wine wagon") at cincybrewbus.com or the Craft Connection Brewery Tours at www.craftconnectiontours.com.

Brewpubs

Given Cincinnati's history with breweries, it is appropriate that its future seems to be linked with beer again, this time in the form of microbreweries and gastropubs. Cincinnati now boasts almost twenty microbreweries, with more popping up monthly, it seems. Accordingly, gastropubs have become the latest popular form of eatery.

What's the difference? It's a fuzzy line, but for the most part, microbreweries focus on the beer—specifically their own. Gastropubs and brewpubs focus on the food *and* the beer. A good brewpub will have about twenty beers on tap, which might rotate in and out according to the brewers' whims and success. Some gastropubs are hooking up with microbreweries so their guests get the best of both worlds.

Now the difference between a brewpub and a restaurant with a bar is that the former serves mostly craft beers, often local, produced in small batches. The latter serves a variety of brews from local, national and international breweries, as well as an assortment of other liquors. A great example of a restaurant with a bar and a good beer selection in Cincinnati is Allyn's Café, on Columbia Parkway. Allyn's (owned by chef Allyn Raifstanger) specializes in Cajun/Creole soul food and has won many awards for both its food and drinks.

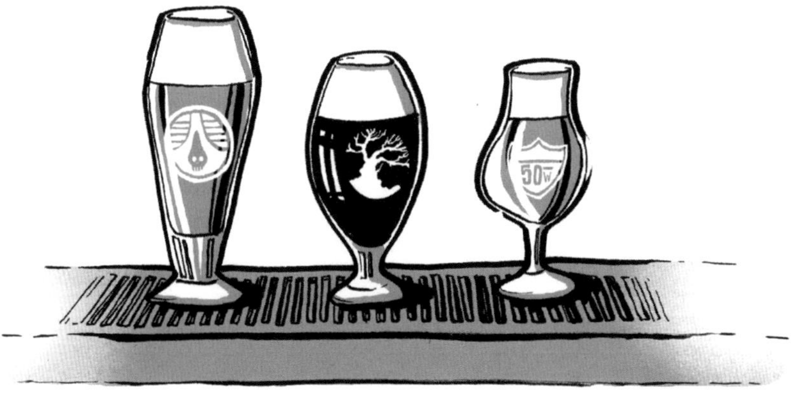

Beer crafting and consuming has become an art in Cincinnati. *Illustration by Allison Ranieri.*

In Cincinnati, the leader of the brewpub craze was, arguably, Rock Bottom Brewery. It's a chain, so some might question its inclusion here, but it did debut the genre of the microbrewery with food in 1991. Here's a bit of trivia: its name comes from the fact that the first Rock Bottom was at the bottom of the building of a certain insurance company whose slogan was "Get a piece of the rock."

The microbrewery experience was further enhanced when the Ohio state legislature passed a bill in 2016 that eliminated the limit on alcohol content in beer to 12 percent. This limit was set in 2002, when there weren't so many microbreweries. The limit put local brewers at a disadvantage, as the surrounding states have no such limit.[62]

In the last decade, brewpubs have appeared all over town. Many have "tap takeovers" when a specific brewery takes over a pub, with its brews as the main feature. It's a good way for patrons to sample many of the brewery's beers. To create your own microbrewery and/or brewpub tour, check out the Beer Guide to Cincinnati, available at www.beeradvocate.com/place/city/39.

TACOS

Cincinnati, despite its Irish-German roots, has a rich past and future with the Latino culture. In addition to the usual plastic pico palaces, Cincinnati's restaurants offer a variety of Tex-Mex fare. The changing demographics, along with many people relocating from Latin American countries, have expanded Cincinnati's palate.

Mazunte Taqueria is one example of a Mexican restaurant that offers more authentic Mexican food than is traditionally offered in the United States and in a more traditional Mexican setting. Situated in Madisonville but named for the Mexican town of Mazunte, the restaurant has the flavor and feel of a Mexican street. Its offerings, *los antojitos*, represent "little cravings" of street food. Although the menu is a little limited, it makes up for the lack of quantity with quality. While you're there, check out the huge margarita drink mixer (but don't help yourself). If you go, be prepared for a wait.

Before Mazunte opened, another restaurant offered Mexican tacos in Over-the-Rhine. Bakersfield, on Vine Street, is a great place to go if you have the time to spare. Like Mazunte, you're going to wait in line. But it's worth the wait when you get a seat. Bakersfield is known for three things: fantastic tacos (small, but they're mighty), an impressive bourbon collection and a flash back to our black-and-white past on the multiple flat-screen televisions around the bar. These TVs play a continuous loop of old westerns—without the sound. If you're lucky enough to be there when my husband and I are dining, he'll recite all the dialogue for you, if you wish.

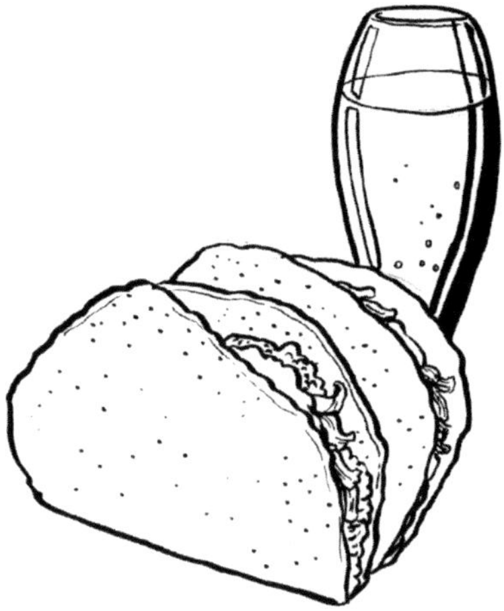

Authentic Mexican restaurants are popping up all over the city. *Illustration by Allison Ranieri.*

Another downtown Latino eatery is Nada, on Walnut Street. It serves Mexican food with a contemporary flair. One of its offerings, for example, is the Mexican poutine—a new take on a Canadian classic. They offer brunch, lunch and dinner, but more importantly, they offer fantastic desserts and signature drinks.

If you want the Mexican without the flash, try Avocado's in Cheviot, on the west side of town. Think of Avocado's as offering down-home Mexican cooking. Like Mazunte, it has a gigantic "slushy" machine filled with margarita. If that's what you're in the mood for, there's no wait. Avocado's offers indoor and outdoor seating, as does Mazunte.

All we need next is a goetta taco.

GOETTA

When people visit Cincinnati, they often ask to be wined and dined at the host's favorite chili parlor and ice cream shop. True Cincinnatians (by birth or at heart) also treat their guests to Cincinnati's finest fare: goetta.

Now pronounced GET-tuh, in the original German it might have been spelled "götte" and pronounced more like "GEU-tteh." Darwin scholar John van Wyhe, a Bye-Fellow of Christ's College and a member of the British Society for the History of Science, expressed the opinion that our word "goetta" sounds like the German slang word *gute*, which means "goody."[63]

This is not his area of expertise, but he's a very smart person. Another smart person whose area of expertise *is* food, Rita Nader Heikenfeld, says that she thinks the name might derive from the German word for grain or cereal.[64]

Some families have handed down their own goetta recipes for generations. The variations are endless, but the basic recipe usually calls for pork (shoulder or butt), pin oats (also called "steel cut"), onion, sometimes a bay leaf and spices. Similar to the spice variations for Cincinnati chili (which isn't really Greek), the spices differ by recipe for goetta (which isn't really German). The exact spices might depend on what part of the old country the recipe creator came from. "Food etymologist" Dann Woellert has tracked the use of specific spices in goetta recipes to different quadrants of Germany. The spices might include allspice and cloves or a more savory combination of marjoram and sage.

The meats can vary, too, but not as much as the spices. Of course, we here in Porkopolis use mostly pork, but sometimes this is augmented by beef. Some recipes include organ meat, while others avoid it. Regardless of what exactly goes in the pot, the hot concoction is simmered for a couple of hours and then packed into pans or sausage casings and chilled.

Goetta is not unique, although we'd like to think so. It is a twist on a common sausage-type food found in areas of the United States with German roots, as well as Europe. Pennsylvanians love their scrapple, which has a similar mixture of meats and spices but uses cornmeal instead of oats. In Europe, the Scots love their haggis, which has a similar mix of grains and spices but uses sheep for the meat. (Haggis has its own debate going on, as England and Scotland are thought of as the country of

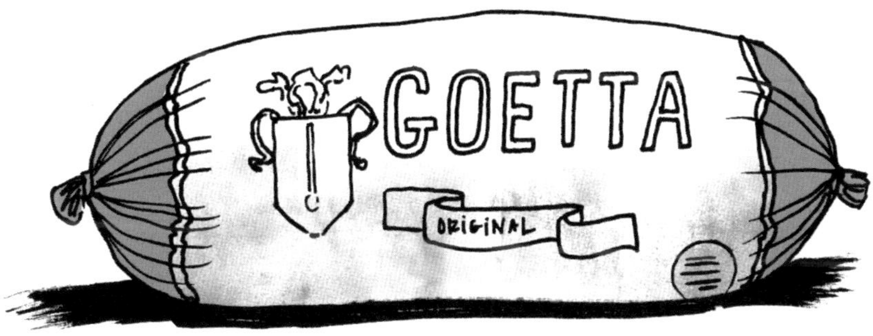

Goetta seems to be a food unique to Cincinnati and northern Kentucky, where Goettafest is celebrated with gusto. *Illustration by Allison Ranieri.*

origin.) Grutzwurt, which hails from northern Germany, is called "kishka" in nearby Poland.[65] The former uses oat groats and organ meat, whereas the latter uses buckwheat, barley or rye. Many cooks in many countries have stretched the meat by adding some grain and grinding it up.

From this description, however, one might get the impression that goetta is strictly a step up from tinned meat. Some people might agree—but not in mixed company.

One local manufacturer, Glier's, hosts Goettafest every August in Newport, Kentucky. You'll get to sample goetta pizza, calzones, Coneys, rangoon, fried rice, spring rolls, doughnuts, brownies, omelets, kabob, macaroni and cheese, burritos, lasagna, risotto balls and even bread pudding. Mainstrasse Village in Covington, Kentucky, also holds a Goettafest in June, so you can double up on your goetta quota.

Many of the traditional butcher shops, like Humbert's Meats, make their goetta right in the store. If you're feeling brave, try one of these two old recipes from my husband's family.

Catherine Grathwohl's Goetta

This recipe comes from my husband's maternal grandmother.

5 cups water
2½ cups pinhead oatmeal (or look for steel-cut oats)
3 teaspoons salt
⅛ teaspoon pepper
1 large onion, finely chopped
1 pound ground pork
1 pound ground beef
1 teaspoon instant beef bouillon
3 bay leaves
¼ teaspoon ground allspice (optional)
¼ teaspoon ground cloves (optional)

Put water, oats, salt and pepper in a slow cooker. Mix well, cover and cook for 1½ hours on high setting. Add onion, meat, bouillon, bay leaves and other spices (if desired). Cook 5 hours on low setting. Remove cover and cook for 30 minutes longer, stirring three or four times. Put cooked goetta in two foil-lined loaf pans and chill. Invert onto plate and chill another 30 minutes. Wrap loaves in foil and store in refrigerator. To serve, slice and fry until crisp and golden. If slow cooker is not available, put ingredients in an oven roaster and bake at 250 degrees for 1 hour with the lid on and 1 hour with the lid off, stirring every half hour.

Notes from Catherine: "Recipe calls for first end of callie [pork shoulder], which I have never been able to get, so I use back and get more than 2 pounds to allow for bone. Pork should not be lean. Do not remove fat but grind it all. The only place I have found oatmeal is at a health store. It is called steel-cut or steel-ground oatmeal. Do *not* use rolled oats."

Matilda "Tilly" Beckman's Goetta

This recipe comes from my husband's paternal great-grandmother, who was married to Leo Beckman.
Serves "lots"

2 pounds fresh pork (not too lean)
½ pound stew beef

Boil together in 6 cups of water and 2 teaspoons salt until tender; remove and allow to cool. While liquid is cooling, grind the meats, including the fat. Strain liquid; if not 6 full cups, add enough water to make that amount. Bring liquid to boil with 2 more teaspoons salt. Add 2 cups oats (*not* rolled oats) slowly. Turn to very low light. Stir frequently until thickened, about 15–20 minutes. Add ground meat to cooked oatmeal and simmer until done, about an hour or so. Watch so it does not stick. Do not put lid on tight because steam should escape. Stir frequently. To serve, slice cold and brown in skillet.

CHAPTER 6

GEOGRAPHY AND NATURAL WONDERS

CINCINNATI ZOO AND BOTANICAL GARDEN

In the mid- to late nineteenth century, Cincinnati had a caterpillar problem. Andrew Erkenbrecher and a handful of other businessmen decided that the local birds were failing to get rid of the intruding insects, so in 1872, they got an ingenious idea. If our local birds were looking down their beaks at the idea of eating these marauding bugs, then they would bring in some foreign birds to do the job for them. Erkenbrecher ordered from Europe a collection of birds, including starlings and English sparrows (which, as it turns out, are neither English nor sparrows; they're finches), to take care of the growing caterpillar problem.

Erkenbrecher and associates also fed the birds, which seems as if it would decrease the birds' appetites. The birds loved the arrangement and agreeably multiplied. Erkenbrecher created the Society for the Acclimatization of Birds and housed the birds in Burnet Woods. Other cities around the world—Moscow, London and Berlin—followed Erkenbrecher's lead. Erkenbrecher eventually released the birds to breed on their own in the wild, much to the chagrin of future Cincinnati bird-watchers,

Erkenbrecher formed the Zoological Society of Cincinnati in 1873 and the next year chose a site of sixty-six and a half acres in Blakely Woods to lease for the site of a new zoo. The zoo officially opened on September 18, 1875, and is the second-oldest zoo in the country, a year behind Philadelphia's.

The initial collection featured more than four hundred birds, eight monkeys, six raccoons, three deer, two grizzly bears, two elk, a buffalo, a hyena, a tiger, a circus elephant and an alligator. At least one of the birds was a talking crow.

Since then, the zoo has had many important—even *nationally* significant—milestones.

Firsts

In 1875, the zoo opened its doors, charging twenty-five cents for adults and fifteen cents for children. The first-ever sea lion was born in captivity in 1878. Two years later, the zoo celebrated the first trumpeter swan ever born in captivity. The first American bison was born in captivity in 1882. The zoo acquired Susie, its first gorilla, in 1931. (She died in 1947 at the age of twenty-two, the oldest gorilla in captivity.) In 1970, Sam was the first gorilla born at the zoo; eight days later, Samantha was born.

The Research Department opened in 1981, and the first artificial insemination of an exotic feline species (Persian leopard) successfully occurred. The next year, the zoo opened a cryogenics unit and began freezing and storing embryos, eggs and semen. The zoo was given the one-hundred-acre Anna Mast Farm for breeding. The first banded linsang born in captivity in the United States was born in the Cincinnati Zoo in 1989. Most recently, Bibi, a Nile hippo on loan from St. Louis, gave birth to her first offspring. Named Fiona, the baby arrived prematurely but thrived, thanks to the care of workers from both the Cincinnati Zoo and Cincinnati Children's Medical Center. Fiona was the first hippo born at the zoo in seventy-five years.

Lasts

Despite the 1880 birth of four passenger pigeons, in 1914 the last surviving passenger pigeon, Martha, died. Her body was immediately frozen and shipped to the Smithsonian Institution in Washington, D.C. In 1918, there was another loss as the world's last surviving Carolina parakeet, Incas, died.

Rarities

In 1888, the zoo acquired Mr. and Mrs. Rooney, thought to be the only captive chimpanzees in the nation at the time. The Cincinnati Summer Opera (known as Zoo Opera) debuted at the zoo in 1920. In 1923, the zoo acquired an alligator that had been raised by a Cincinnati family. Almost seventy years later, Tojo was recognized as the oldest alligator in captivity. In 1957, Dr. Albert Schweitzer donated a three-year-old gorilla named Penelope to the children of Cincinnati; she was later given to the zoo. *Newsweek* magazine called the Cincinnati Zoo the "sexiest zoo in the country" in 1974 for its successful breeding practices, such as holding the records for gorilla births and black rhino births, and for being one of only five zoos in the world to successfully breed Komodo dragons. The Komodo

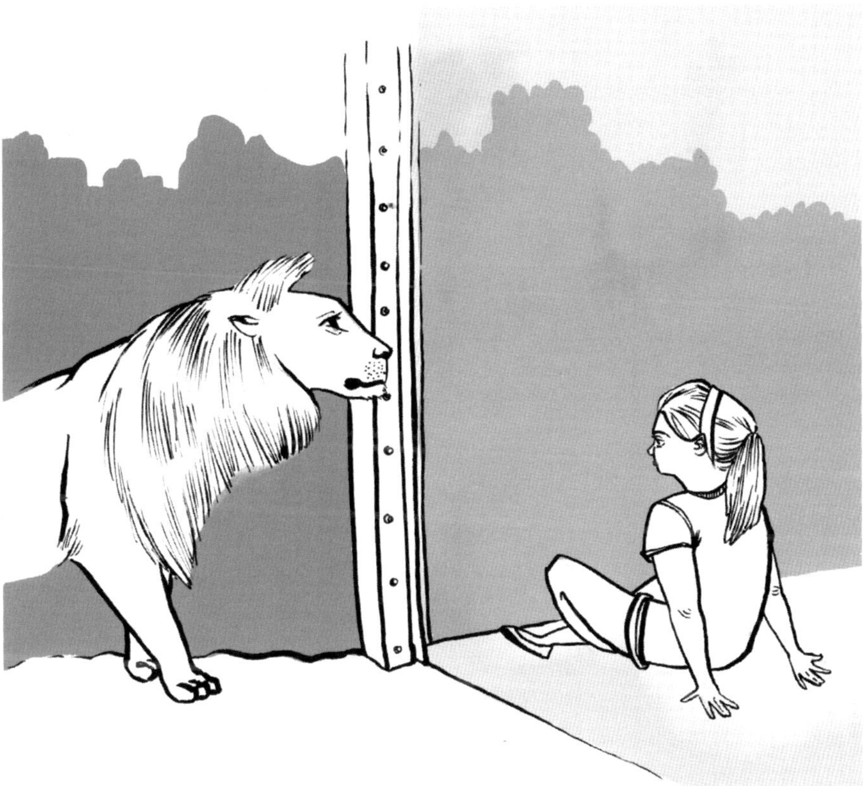

The Cincinnati Zoo and Botanical Garden provides education and entertainment. *Illustration by Allison Ranieri.*

dragon exhibit opened in 1990 with President George Herbert Walker Bush's donation of Naga, which had been a gift from the government of Indonesia. The Botanical Center and Oriental Garden also opened that year. In 1991, the Carl H. Lindner Center for the Reproduction of Endangered Wildlife (CREW) was dedicated. Four years later, the zoo set a U.S. record with six gorilla births in one year, including the world's first test-tube gorilla.

In 2011, Cincinnati celebrated the birth—and then mourned the death three months later—of Zuri the giraffe. The next year, the city mourned the death of Ipuh, a thirty-three-year-old Sumatran rhino, believed to be the oldest such rhino in captivity. Giraffe lovers were heartened by the birth of another baby Masai giraffe, Lulu. An eleven-year-old cheetah named Sarah set a new record for the fastest land mammal by running the one-hundred-meter dash in 5.95 seconds. She accomplished this feat while filming for a *National Geographic* magazine shoot. Her top speed was sixty-one miles per hour. The Cincinnati Zoo was chosen as the ideal home for baby Gladys, a Western Lowland gorilla that was born in January 2013 but was then rejected by her mother. A team of ten human surrogate "mothers" wearing special furs worked around the clock to assist in Gladys's "gorillification" until she could make the transition to a real gorilla surrogate.[66]

The Cincinnati Zoo and Botanical Garden is open every day of the year except December 25. It opens all other days at 10:00 a.m., with certain early-entry days for members. Find out more at cincinnatizoo.org.

Eden Park

At age twenty-one, Nicholas Longworth came to Cincinnati in 1804 to work as a law student in the office of Judge Jacob Burnet, brother of Mayor Isaac Burnet. "Nick" Longworth didn't stay with Judge Burnet for very long, though, as he had been bitten by the real estate bug. He had a keen eye for the potential value of land and began to buy up every little parcel he could, no matter how small and no matter who had rejected it.

One favorite story told by Nick Longworth and his contemporaries was about his defending an alleged horse stealer. After Longworth got the man acquitted, the man was allowed to keep the horse he was accused of stealing. Immensely grateful, the former alleged horse thief offered Longworth one or two (the story varied) of his moonshine stills as payment. However, when Longworth went to collect, the stills were not there; some "worthless" acreage along Western Row in downtown Cincinnati was offered instead. Longworth snatched up the property.

By 1859, the land was worth $750,000; its value soon shot into the millions. Longworth became enamored of the arts of grape growing and winemaking and found much of his new land perfect for these pursuits. Longworth, at this point, had more money, owned more land and produced more wine than anyone else in the country.

Not only did Longworth have a keen real estate acumen, but he also had a deep passion for flora and fauna. A Maryland botanist named John Adlum gave Longworth his first grapevines. Adlum often joked that if Longworth were thrown into the Ohio River, he would bob to the surface clutching a rare species of fish in one hand and a freshwater pearl in the other.[67]

Besides land and nature, Longworth also especially appreciated the fruits of the vine, specifically grapes. He developed an interest in the native Catawba grape after a friend gave him a vine sample, so he reinvented himself as a vintner. At his vineyards' peak, his vines covered more than three thousand acres, producing more than 550,000 gallons of sparkling wine.

He gave poet Henry Wadsworth Longfellow a case of Catawba wine. Longfellow then wrote an homage to the wine, the vine and the vintner, closing with the following:

While pure as a spring
Is the wine I sing,
And to praise it, one needs but name it;
For Catawba wine
Has need of no sign,
No tavern-bush to proclaim it.

And this Song of the Vine,
This greeting of mine,
The winds and the birds shall deliver
To the Queen of the West,
In her garlands dressed,
On the banks of the Beautiful River.

Although Cincinnati's breweries were just taking off in the middle of the nineteenth century, the Ohio wine industry was decreasing. It hit its

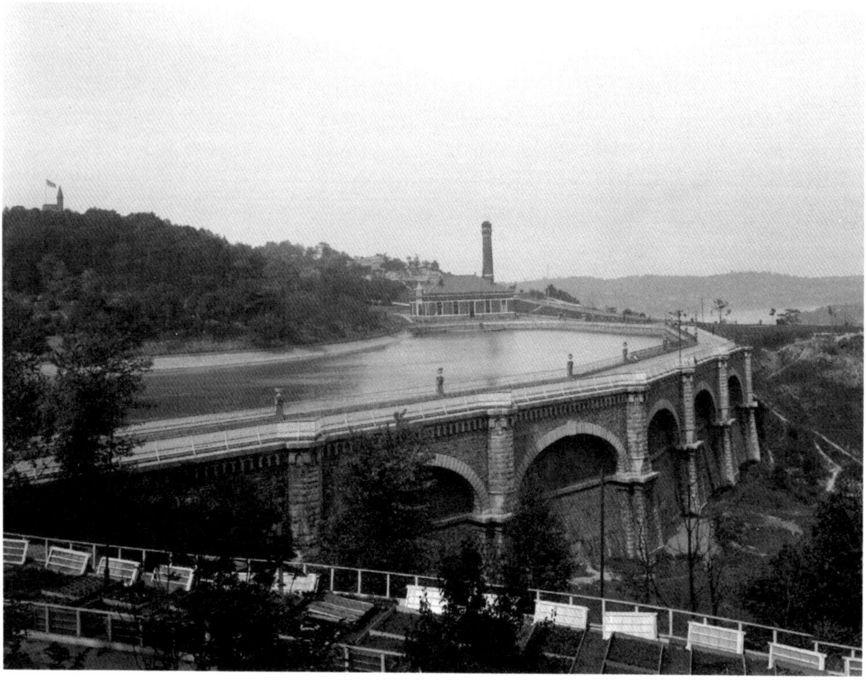

The reservoirs at Eden Park (east basin, seen here) served a vital purpose for the citizens of Cincinnati. *Library of Congress.*

peak in 1859, producing 568,000 gallons of wine, most of it Catawba. Rumors of even better land for the Catawba grape farther north in Ohio never bore fruit.

Nicholas Longworth spent his last days at Rookwood, on Grandin Road. By then, powder mildew and black rot were hitting many vineyards hard, wiping out entire crops. Longworth spent his final days looking for another grape that might better withstand the rot. His final words were for W.J. Flagg, his vintner son-in-law. Just before slipping into unconsciousness, he asked if Flagg had arrived. He wanted to tell him of a new vine he had found that was resistant to mildew and rot. Nicholas Longworth died on February 10, 1863, at the age of eighty.

Despite attempts to save them, Longworth's beloved vineyards died off from blight. The land was then donated by his son, Joseph, to the City of Cincinnati to become the foundation of Eden Park.[68]

To this day, Eden Park is a haven atop one of Cincinnati's tallest hills. It boasts the Cincinnati Art Museum, the Krohn Conservatory, the Murray

Seasongood Pavilion and the Cincinnati Playhouse in the Park. Two reservoirs that once provided water to the city were co-opted for more modern use. The lower (east) basin was dismantled in the 1960s and turned into ball fields. The upper basin was partially filled in to become a reflecting pool named Mirror Lake, a favorite destination of dog walkers and nature watchers.

KROHN CONSERVATORY

Mention "city parks" and trails, rivers and playgrounds might come to mind. One of the Cincinnati City Parks is a building: Krohn Conservatory. It was built in 1933 and shows hints of the Art Deco movement that was so prevalent in Cincinnati at that time. The conservatory was originally a greenhouse, with aluminum and glass walls.

Step into the conservatory and you're instantly transported to a lush tropical environment (complete with an indoor waterfall) with thousands of plant species, including a special bonsai exhibit. Various exhibitions rotate through Krohn Conservatory, but two stand out. Each year in the

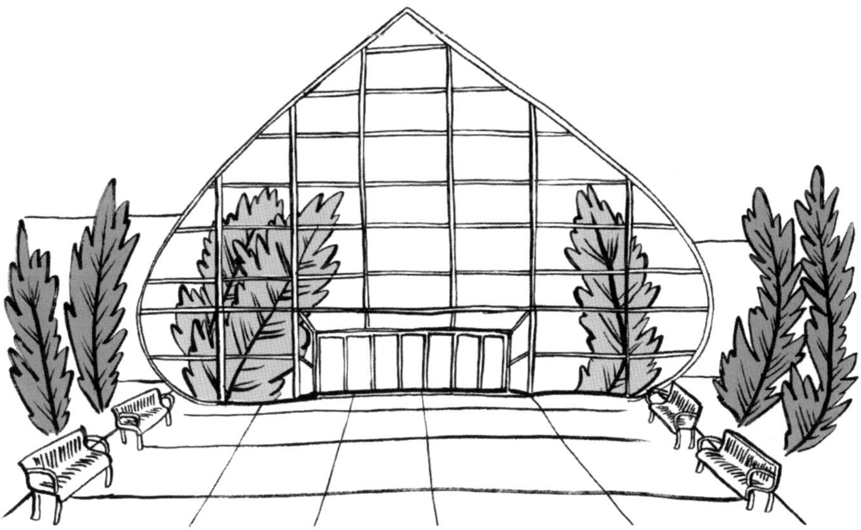

The Krohn Conservatory is open year round but is especially popular during its winter and spring butterfly exhibits. *Illustration by Allison Ranieri.*

spring, the conservatory holds a spectacular butterfly show. Butterflies from all over the world delight adults and youth alike. One of the best treats is to sit still and see what butterflies alight. Make sure to wear bright colors! At the other end of the year, the Krohn often creates a nativity scene, complete with live animals.

The conservatory can be reserved for private functions—even weddings. Prices and hours of regular admission depend on the exhibit, so check out the website before you go: www.cincinnatiparks.com/krohn-conservatory.

Cincinnati Parks

Cincinnati has been recognized as one of the greenest cities in the United States, thanks to its many Cincinnati City Parks and Hamilton County Parks. Activities at these parks include hiking, fishing, meeting butterflies, playing and much more. The Cincinnati Park Board manages almost fifty facilities in all parts of the city. Several of the parks are along the Ohio: Smale Riverfront Park, downtown, has a merry-go-round; Sawyer Point and Yeatman's Cove are especially popular during Riverfest; and Theodore M. Berry International Friendship Park offers bike rental for riding along the river.

The Trust for Public Land has rated the City of Cincinnati's Park system "excellent" for finding funding sources for the conservation and

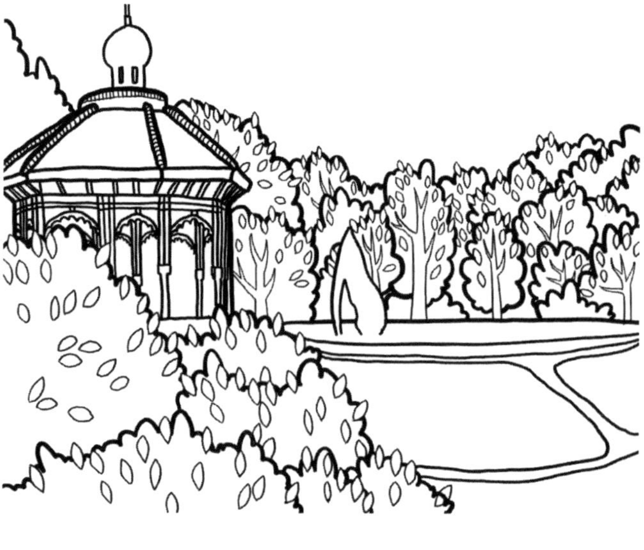

Cincinnati's city parks make it one of the greenest cities in the United States. *Illustration by Allison Ranieri.*

maintenance of the city's parks. The park system includes a 1,459-acre forest, five nature centers, an arboretum and Krohn Conservatory, one of the largest public plant conservatories in the nation.[69]

Besides the City Park System, Cincinnati is also blessed with the "Great Parks of Hamilton County," founded in 1930 as the Hamilton County Park District. The parks offer opportunities for such things as fishing (some catch and release, some catch and eat), play areas for sports, dog parks, forest preserves, hiking, horseback riding, camping, picnicking and even a historic village. More than seventeen thousand acres are available 365 days a year, from dawn to dusk, for enjoyment and education. A yearly motor vehicle permit is available at a small price, with discounts for Hamilton County residents and members of the armed services. For more information, visit www.greatparks.org.

Fossiliferous Limestone

More than 400 million years ago, a shallow inland sea covered what we today call Cincinnati. But for now, we'll call it "Crinoid City," for this sea was full of marine animals like brachiopods, coral, bryozoans and the tulip-like crinoids. When these ancient animals died, their calcium-rich shells became part of the fossiliferous limestone found today in many Cincinnatians' mantels, retaining walls and garden walkways. In fact, Cincinnati has the best fossils in the world from this phase of geologic time, known as the Ordovician Period. If it weren't for our natural humility, this age might have been named the "Cincinnatian Period" instead.

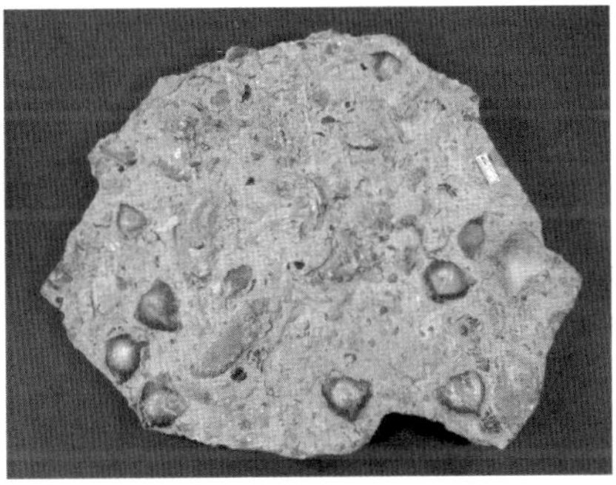

This fossil slab, from the Cincinnatian Series of the late Ordovician Period, has several major fossil groups on it: trilobites, brachiopods, bryozoans, crinoid stems and clams. *Professor David Meyer, UC Department of Geology.*

Skipping from the crinoids of the Paleozoic Era to the Pleistocene Period in the Cenozoic Era, at a time approximately one million years ago, there were still no humans. But there were glaciers—the Kansan, the Illinoian and the Wisconsinan. These three glaciers carved out the valleys and hills that made Cincinnati what it is today, topographically. Prior to that, the main body of water (called the Teays River by geologists) flowed north, which is why the Licking River flows north. Just as the Licking fed the Teays, the Licking now feeds the Ohio.

The city lies in the bottom of a bowl surrounded by the hills that were shaped by these great geological forces of nature. The bowl was also created by the confluence of the Licking, Ohio, Little Miami and Great Miami Rivers. The sides of the bowl serve as a natural windbreak, making the Ohio Valley a catch basin for allergens and airborne particulates. Thanks to its hills, Cincinnati has earned one of its other nicknames: "the sinus capital of the world."[70]

Cincinnati Observatory

The quest for a national observatory was led by John Quincy Adams, the new sixth president of the United States (after Washington, his father, Jefferson, Madison and Monroe). He wished for an observatory that was affiliated with a university well founded in science.

Adams said he was "less possessed of your confidence in advance than any of my predecessors," but he promised to make up for this with "intentions upright and pure, a heart devoted to the welfare of our country, and the unceasing application of all the faculties allotted to me to her service."

Adams advocated a system of internal improvements (mostly canals and turnpikes) to be paid for out of increasing revenues from western land sales and a continuing tariff on imports. He called for the establishment of a uniform system of weights and measures and the improvement of the patent system, both to promote science and to encourage a spirit of enterprise and invention in the United States.

In a further effort to support science and spread its benefits to the nation and the world, he advocated an extensive survey of the nation's own coasts, land and resources. John Quincy Adams urged the building of an astronomical observatory ("lighthouses of the skies") so the United States could make at least one such contribution to the advancement of knowledge to supplement the 130 observatories that had already been constructed in Europe.[71]

Enter Ormsby MacKnight Mitchel, born in Kentucky on August 28 (1809 or 1810) and raised in Lebanon, Ohio. He went to West Point, where he was a classmate of Robert E. Lee and graduated fifteenth out of forty-six. He stayed on at West Point as a math professor, later becoming a lawyer.

Years later, Mitchel approached fellow attorney Nicholas Longworth for a donation to help build the nation's first observatory. Instead of giving them some money, Longworth surprised them by donating four acres of land on top of what was then known as Mount Ida.

Former president John Quincy Adams spread the first layer of mortar and laid the cornerstone on November 9, 1843, declaring the occasion a tribute to the citizens of Cincinnati and an example to the rest of the nation. The seventy-six-year-old Adams braved failing health to make the trip because of his commitment to science and his dedication to the idea of a national observatory. (The event was Adams's last public speech before his death in 1848.) When the Cincinnati Observatory was completed in June 1845, it was the first in the nation. Mount Ida was renamed Mount Adams, in honor of the former president who had felt it was so important to make the trip to Cincinnati.

In 1859, Mitchel became the astronomer of Dudley Observatory in Albany. He commanded the Department of the Ohio in the Civil War from September to November 1861. He led the failed but famous plan to steal a train in Georgia and then died from yellow fever in September 1862.

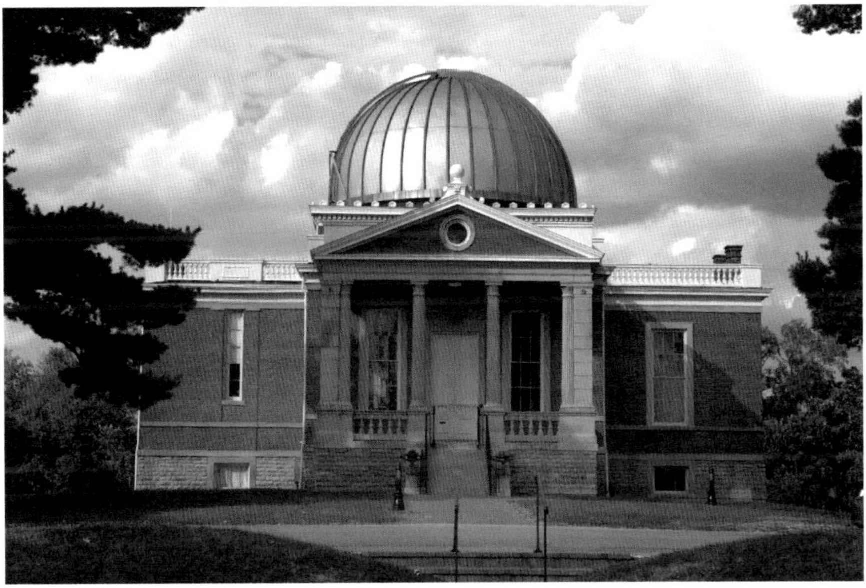

One of two buildings at the Cincinnati Observatory, sometimes called the "Birthplace of American Astronomy." *Carol M. Highsmith, Library of Congress.*

In the observatory's 170-plus years of operation, it has had nine directors: Ormsby MacKnight Mitchel, Henry Twitchell, Cleveland Abbe, Ormand Stone, Jermain Gildersleeve Porter,[72] Everett I. Yowell, Elliot S. Smith, Paul Herget and Craig Niemi.

Today, the mission of the Cincinnati Observatory is to maintain the integrity and heritage of a historic nineteenth-century observatory while promoting the study and practice of twenty-first-century astronomy and science. Its vision is to be a primary resource in furthering astronomy and science education through programming for K–12 schools and the public on and off its campus, for universities and classes for teacher professional development, to promote the rich history of the observatory and to strengthen the connection to allied STEM (science, technology, engineering and math) organizations.[73] To learn more about the nation's first observatory, visit www.cincinnatiobservatory.org.

"SEVEN" HILLS

Cincinnati is famous for its seven hills. When the city was named for the Society of Cincinnati (honoring Rome's Cincinnatus), it was a natural to compare our seven hills to the seven hills of Rome.

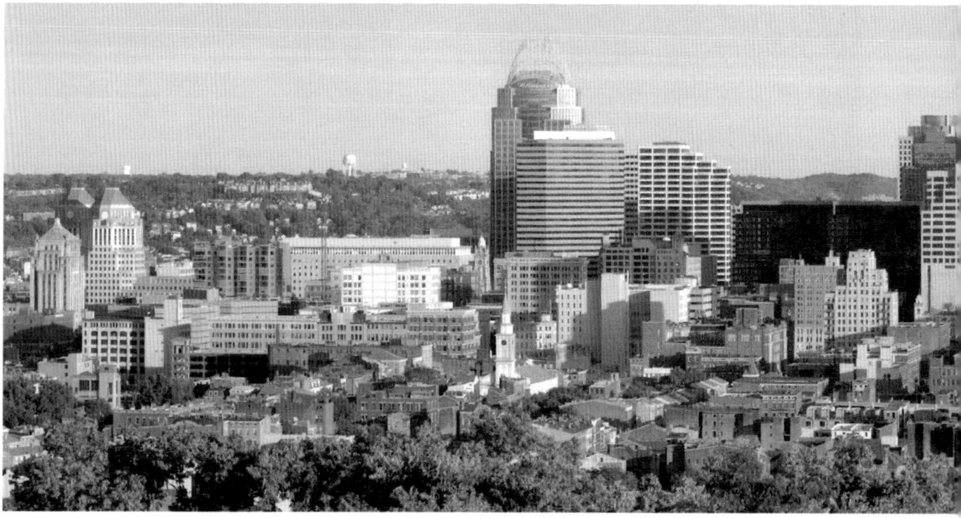

However, ask any Cincinnatian to name the seven hills, and you'll get way more than seven suggestions: Clifton Heights, College Hill, Fairmount, Fairview Heights, Mount Adams, Mount Airy, Mount Auburn, Mount Lookout, Mount Echo, Mount Storm, Mount Healthy, Mount Washington, Price Hill, the Vine Street Hill and Walnut Hills. (The highest of these is Mount Airy, at an elevation of 938 feet above sea level.)[74]

Since Cincinnati has been known for its seven hills for a long time, one theory holds that the original seven were those closest to downtown. The University of Cincinnati library says that the seven hills are Mount Adams, Mount Airy, Mount Echo, Mount Healthy, Mount Lookout, Mount Storm and Mount Washington. According to the *West American Review* 1853 edition, the seven hills were Mount Adams, Walnut Hills, Mount Auburn, the Vine Street Hill, Fairmount, Mount Harrison and College Hill.[75]

For the definitive list of seven hills, Cincinnati guru and "Dry Dredger" Greg Hand should have the last word. On his website, he has compiled all references to Cincinnati's seven hills and the number of times each was mentioned. Here are the top seven winners of this hilly popularity contest, in order from top to bottom: Mount Adams, Mount Auburn, Mount Harrison/Price Hill, Walnut Hills, Fairmount, Mount Lookout and Mount Echo.[76]

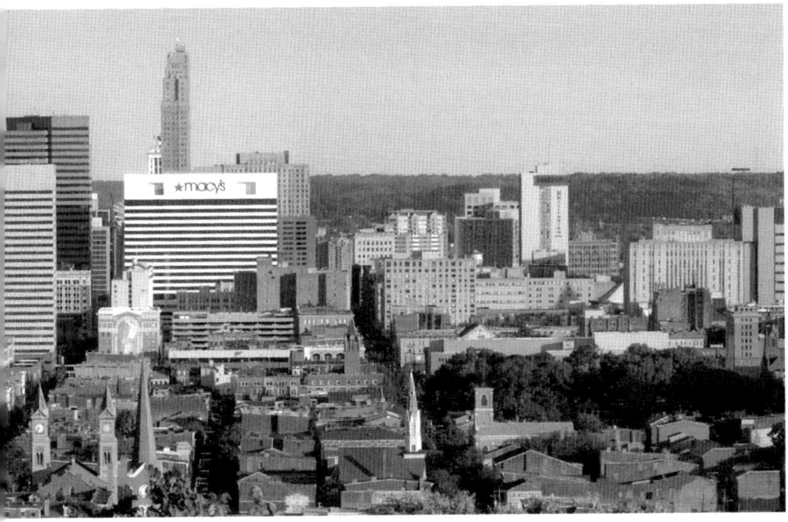

Many Fortune 500 companies have their world headquarters in Cincinnati. *Travis Estell.*

Cincinnati Waterways

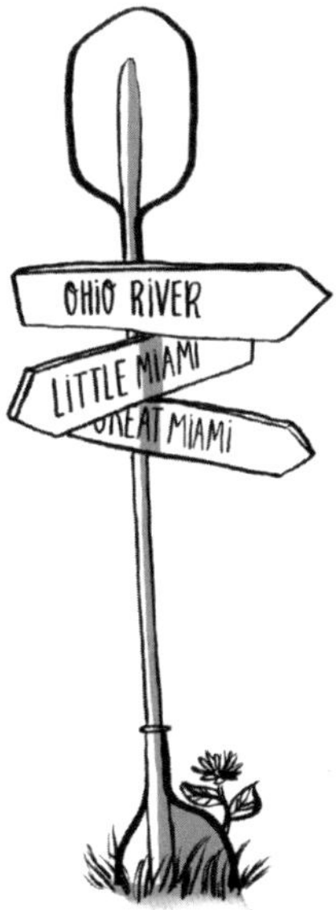

Cincinnati's three rivers play a key role in the life of the city, from economics to entertainment. *Illustration by Allison Ranieri.*

The Ohio River is a distinct landmark in Cincinnati. It serves as the southern border of both the city and the state. That border is right at the water's edge, as the Commonwealth of Kentucky owns the Ohio River. (Well, it owns the river *bottom*.) If an Ohio resident wishes to get married on one of the riverboats, the boat must heave to the Cincinnati side and moor the boat during the "legal" part of the ceremony.

Before the U.S. Army Corps of Engineers deepened the channel, the Ohio River was much shallower than it is now. In 1824, the corps was assigned with clearing the river of snags, sandbars and debris. Still, the natural river depth varied over the course of a year. At some times during the year, the river was barely twelve inches deep. Other times, after melting snow had swelled the river upstream, it swelled to great depths and was nearly impassable.

On July 4, 1825, ground was broken for the Ohio and Erie and Miami and Erie Canals. The Miami and Erie Canal, built from 1825 to 1845 to connect Cincinnati to Lake Erie in Toledo, helped carry Cincinnati's pork products to an even larger, more eager market.

Construction began on the Ohio and Erie Canal in 1825 and concluded by 1833. Cincinnati's portion of the Miami and Erie Canal was completed as far as Middletown by 1829 and as far as Dayton by the 1830s. (However, it took until 1845 to finish the entire stretch to Toledo.) The canal followed what today is called Central Parkway, going south into town. Then it continued east until it ran into what is now Eggleston. From there, it followed Eggleston's path to the Ohio River.

The canals could accommodate a few different types of boats. The barges, the slow beasts of burden, were up to seventy-eight feet long and fourteen feet wide. These boats could carry up to sixty tons of freight and were pulled by horses or mules walking along the bank. The lighter packet boats could seat people above or below deck. Packet boats could carry up to forty people and also carried the mail.

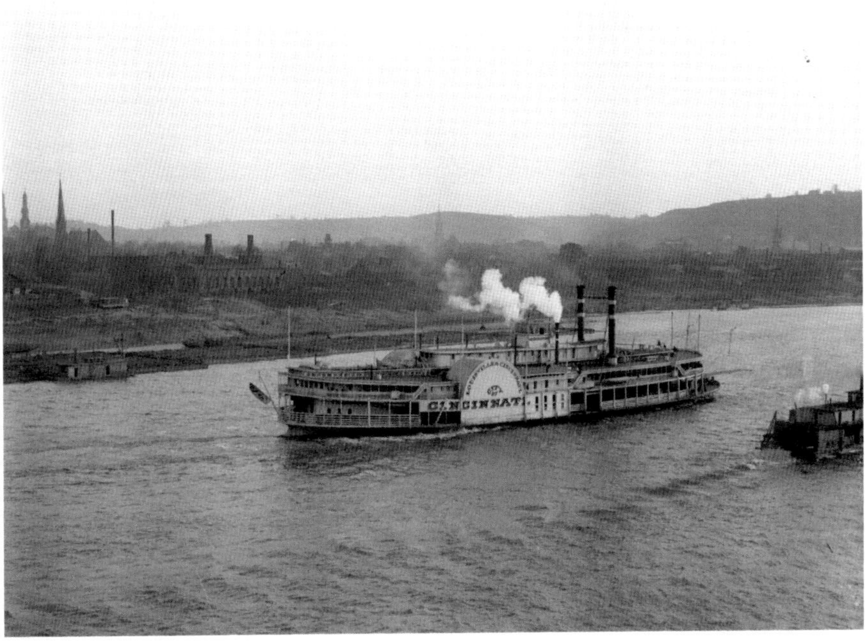

The *City of Cincinnati*, Detroit Publishing Co., 1906. *Library of Congress.*

Cincinnati's canal turned out to offer more than just a means of transportation for businesses. It also provided swimming for youths on hot days and skating on cold ones, water for quenching fires and ice for cooling beer at the many taverns. The canal became an immediate sensation, reducing both the time and cost of transporting Cincinnati's goods to northern markets.

The canal also became known as something else. With an influx of immigrating Germans, the canal must have reminded them of the Rhine, and thus the canal became the border of the neighborhood known as Over-the-Rhine. Unfortunately, the canal is believed to have contributed to the cholera epidemics of the early 1800s.

Cincinnati enjoyed a transportation heyday in the 1840s with the Ohio River, its canal, its roads and its rail. However, Cincinnatians were slow to embrace railroads. Although many north–south routes ran through Cincinnati, east–west routes tended to run north of the city. Goods from the northeastern cities of Boston, New York and Philadelphia were on their way to Cleveland and Chicago, bypassing Cincinnati and its wares. At this point, Cincinnati lost its position as the leader of meatpacking. When, in the 1860s, the Civil War caused the closure of the Ohio River to commercial shipping, Cincinnati's ability to market its goods was further paralyzed.

The Cincinnati stretch of the Miami and Erie Canal was drained into the Ohio River in 1919. At first, the bed of the canal was to be used for a subway in Cincinnati. However, with the growing popularity of the automobile, interest in a rail system waned. The plan was abandoned in 1927 in favor of filling in the canal to become a street, and in 1928, Central Parkway was dedicated.

On the Ohio, steamboats provided both entertainment and transportation. They also faced their share of trouble. The first *Island Queen*, which carried visitors to Coney Island, caught fire at Cincinnati's public landing and burned to the waterline in 1922. (The *Morning Star*, *Island Maid*, *Chris Greene* and *Tacoma* were completely destroyed in the same fire.)

Every three to four years, Cincinnati hosts Tall Stacks, a celebration of the city's musical and nautical heritage featuring a parade of boats. The first festival was held in 1988 to celebrate the city's bicentennial.

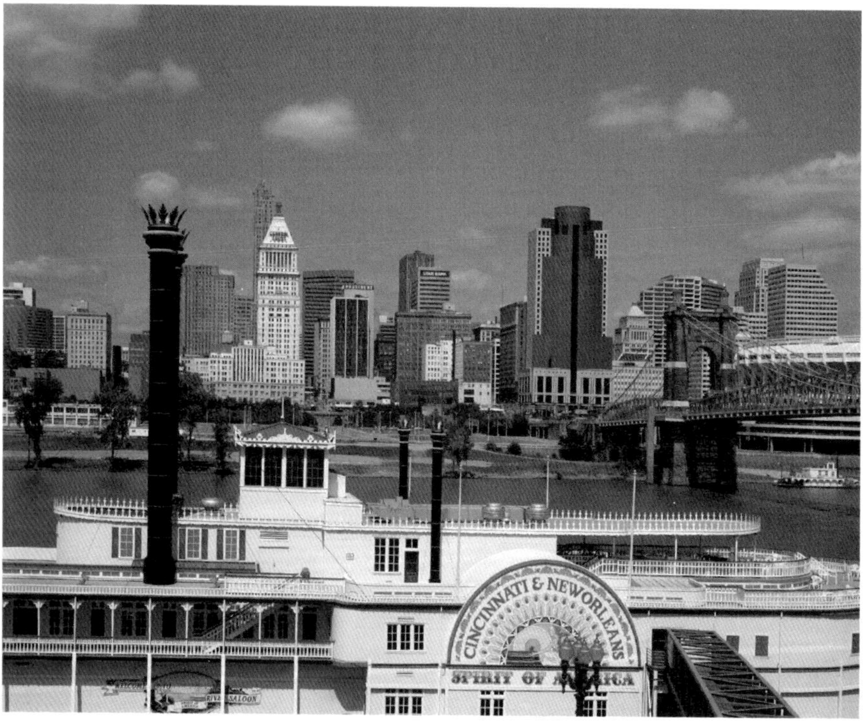

The *Spirit of America* paddleboat enhances the Cincinnati skyline. *Carol M. Highsmith, Library of Congress.*

The Ohio River Paddlefest, held annually in August, draws more than two thousand people from twenty-five states to paddle nine miles of the river. Canoeists and kayakers enjoy viewing both skylines as they paddle under the six bridges. For more information, check out www.ohioriverpaddlefest.org.

These days, cruises are still available on the Ohio through a number of companies. One of the most popular is BB Riverboats. Original owner Ben Bernstein named it "BB" for himself and his friend Betty Blake, a Cincinnati legend. The company's first boat, now retired, was called the *Betty Blake*. Its two boats now used are the three-deck *Belle of Cincinnati* and the two-deck *River Queen*. They feature dinner cruises, ice cream "Social Sundays" and Dixieland jazz cruises.

For more information on many of Cincinnati's cruises, check out the Cincinnati Destination Guide at dguides.com/cincinnati/activities/recreation/riverboat-cruises.

Chapter 7
History

Home of American Reformed Judaism/Isaac Wise

Rabbi Isaac Wise arrived in Cincinnati in 1854 with his wife, Therese, from Albany, New York. In Albany, Wise had already begun to change how Jews practiced their faith. He had dropped the bar mitzvah in favor of confirmation, instituted choral singing and integrated the seating of men and women in the service.

The Cincinnati congregation of B'nai Yeshurun Wise had heard of Wise's national reputation, so it is not surprising that he was invited to preach a guest sermon. However, what *is* surprising is that Wise said he would come only if they named him their permanent pastor, sight unseen. They did, so he came to Cincinnati. He continued his reforms upon his arrival in Cincinnati and being elected rabbi by B'nai Yeshurun.

Although Wise became known as the founder of American Reform Judaism, the orthodox B'nai Israel congregation was without a leader. Despite their different philosophies, they asked Rabbi Wise to lead them also—which he did for a year, until replaced by his friend Rabbi Max Lilienthal.

The twenty-year-old B'nai Yeshurun congregation was composed of about two hundred families. When they decided it was time to build a temple, they solicited Rabbi Wise's input. He told them to build a temple that would fit

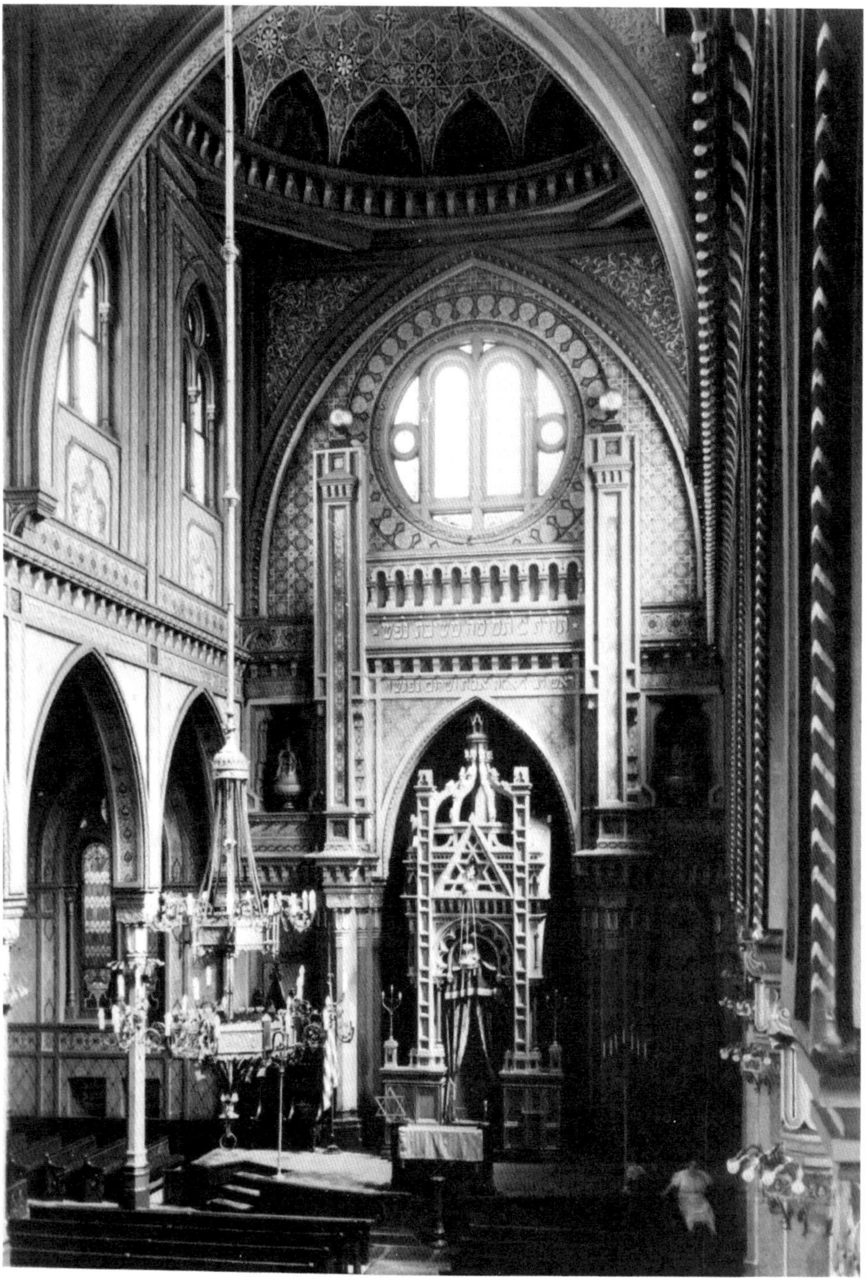

Isaac Wise (Plum) Temple, interior. *Library of Congress.*

one thousand people. He envisioned the congregation and the city as being the beginning of the home of the next Golden Age of Jewish Life.

Cincinnati was Wise's home for the rest of his life. He established the *Israelite* newspaper here (which became the *American Israelite* in 1874 and is still published in Cincinnati today). In 1855, Rabbis Wise and Lilienthal founded Zion College, which became Hebrew Union College twenty years later. It was the first Jewish theological seminary in the United States.

Wise was the father to more than just American Reform Judaism: he was also the biological father of ten children.

Reform Judaism thrives in Cincinnati. In 1972, Sally Priesand was ordained at the Plum Street Temple. She was the first American female rabbi to be ordained by a rabbinical seminary and was only the second female formally ordained in Jewish history.[77]

CINCINNATI REDS

In 1869, the first professional baseball team was established in Cincinnati as the Cincinnati Red Stockings. Then from 1890 to 1953, they were known as the Cincinnati Reds. However, because of the Communist scare, from 1954 to 1959 they became the Cincinnati Redlegs. They finally went back to being our Cincinnati Reds, which they remain today.

From 1876 to 1989, as a tribute to being the first professional team, the Reds were given the honor of opening the Opening Day games; the first two exceptions were 1877 and 1966 because of weather. On April 14, 1910, for the first time, the opening pitch at the Reds game on Opening Day was thrown by the president of the United States: local boy made good William Howard Taft. This tradition continued for many years.

Another U.S. president played a key role in Reds' history in 1935. On May 24, the Reds played the first Major League Baseball game under the lights. Five hundred miles away, President Franklin D. Roosevelt threw the switch in the White House to light Crosley Field. The Reds went on to beat the Philadelphia Phillies, 2–1. The Reds played every National League team at night that year, eight in all. (Incidentally, the minor leagues had been playing night games since 1930.)

Powel Crosley Jr. became majority owner of the Cincinnati Reds baseball team in 1934. He owned the Reds until his death in 1961. Even as majority owner, however, he didn't broadcast the games on his own radio station,

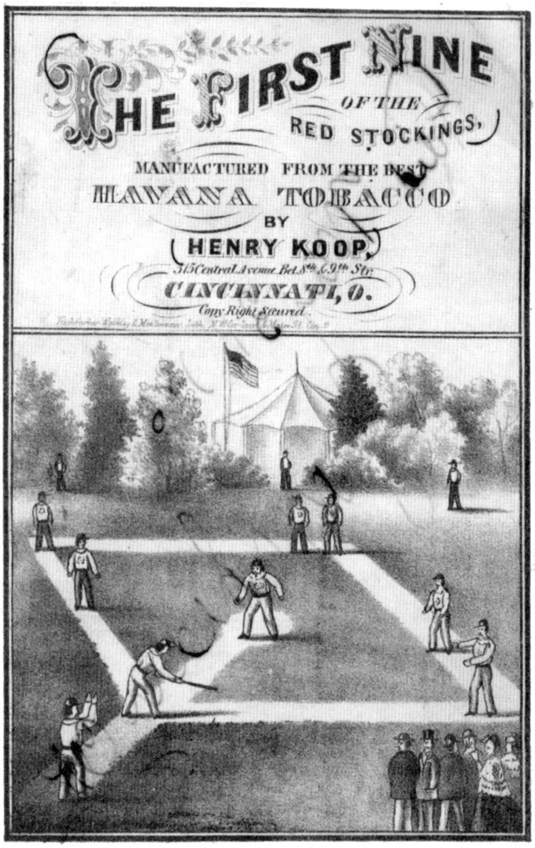

Right: "The first nine of the Red Stockings," manufactured from the best Havana tobacco by Henry Koop. Baseball card printed 1869. *Library of Congress.*

Below: Pete Rose was called "Charlie Hustle" for his head-first slides and the "Hit King" for holding the record for the most lifetime hits: 4,256. *Illustration by Allison Ranieri.*

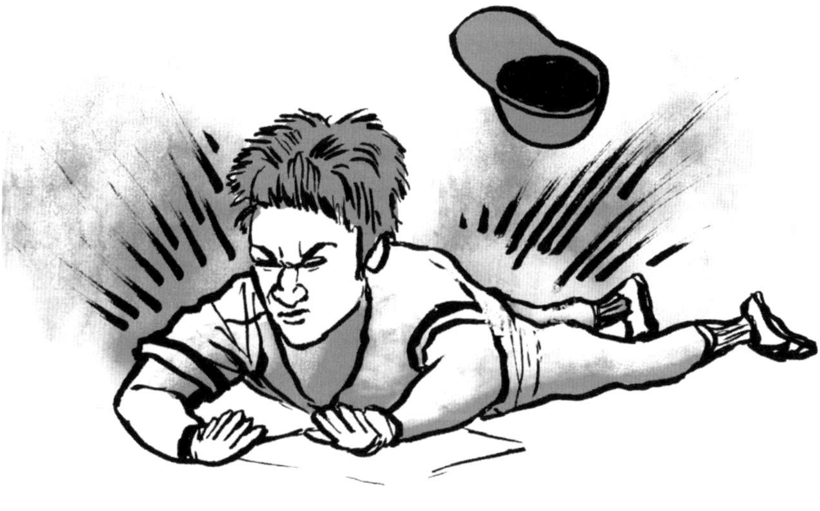

WLW. The baseball owners strongly felt that broadcasting the games would hurt ticket sales. Crosley also didn't want to waste the airtime on WLW, so he carried the games on WSAI, his smaller station.

Crosley bought the Reds to keep them in Cincinnati and to keep them out of bankruptcy. At that point, no Major League Baseball team had moved since 1903, but that was not a guarantee that it couldn't happen with the right offer.

"I have no desire to make money out of the Reds," Crosley said, "and I'm willing to spend money whenever it will keep the club."[78]

When Crosley died in 1961, his name remained only on Crosley Field, the home of the Reds until Riverfront Stadium was completed in 1970. Its successor, Great American Ball Park, now has a Crosley Terrace in his memory.

The owners of the Reds read like a who's who of founding Cincinnatians. With Louis Nippert as the owner, the Cincinnati "Big Red Machine" won back-to-back world championships in 1975 and 1976. Their first "wire-to-wire" season in 1990 was under the ownership of the first woman to own a Major League Baseball team, Marge Schott.[79]

John Roebling Suspension Bridge

Many bridges connect Cincinnati to its southern neighbor. Given whose water they pass over, it should come as no surprise that of the four bridges named for people, three are named for Kentuckians. The fourth proudly bears the name of the builder of the Brooklyn Bridge, John A. Roebling, as a bold reminder that he built *our* suspension bridge first. What might be surprising, however, is that the Roebling Suspension Bridge, the first of the bridges, was built during the Civil War.

Before the war, Cincinnati was the wealthiest northern city that bordered the South. Unfortunately, that was due to a great extent to its proximity to the South. Although in a free state, many Cincinnatians had relatives in the South, wearing the gray and sympathizing with the rebellion. Ohio governor William Dennison was advised to order Columbiads—large-caliber, smoothbore, muzzle-loading cannons that could fire heavy projectiles at both high and low trajectories. These were to be mounted on Cincinnati's hills and aimed at Kentucky. Cincinnatians were conflicted.

A group of Cincinnati leaders visited Kentucky governor Beriah Magoffin to seek his confirmation that Kentucky would do nothing that could be perceived as "menacing." Much discussion followed, both on the state and local level. Governor Dennison wanted to keep trade open between Kentucky and Ohio as long as Kentucky was not in "open rebellion." The nervous people in Cincinnati, however, didn't feel that was good enough. They wanted a promise from Kentucky that the commonwealth would be loyal to the Union or shipping from Ohio would cease.

"This is no time for soft words," said Judge Bellamy Storer. "We feel, as you have a right to feel, that you have a governor who cannot be depended upon in this crisis. But it is on the men of Kentucky that we rely. All we want to know is whether you are for the Union, without reservation. Brethren of Kentucky! The men of the North have been your friends, and they still desire to be. But I will speak plainly....There is a point which cannot be passed. While we rejoice in your friendship, while we glory in your bravery, we would have you understand that we are your equals as well as your friends."

Although Kentucky assured the Cincinnati men that they wanted no part in the war, they were pleased with Governor Dennison's view. The Cincinnatians were not; they gathered four days later to pass the following: "*Resolved* that any men or set of men in Cincinnati or elsewhere, who knowingly sell or ship one ounce of flour or pound of provisions, or any

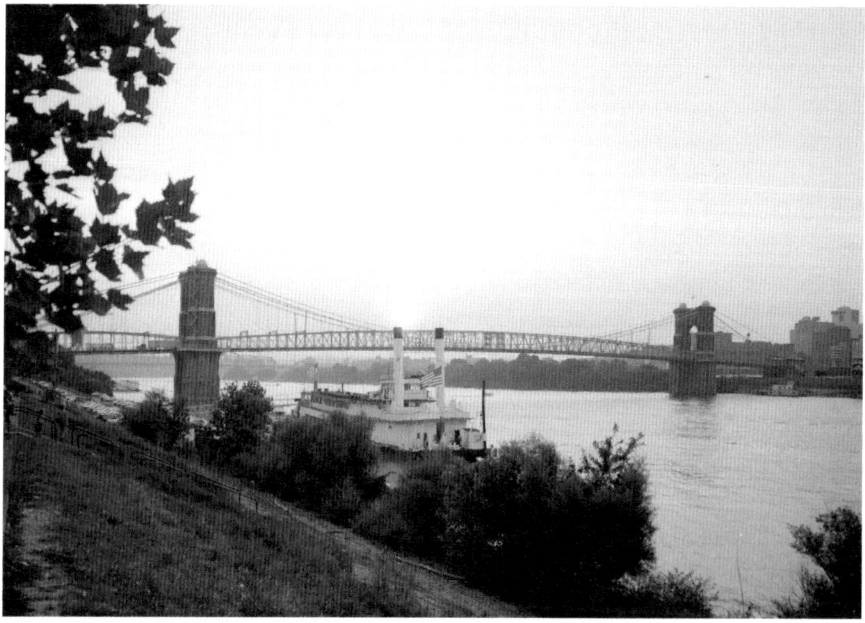

The John Roebling Suspension Bridge was the prototype for New York's Brooklyn Bridge. *Library of Congress.*

arms or articles which are contraband of war, to any person or any State which has not declared its firm determination to sustain the Government in the present crisis, is a traitor, and deserves the doom of a traitor."[80]

Despite the chaos going on around it, the Covington and Cincinnati Suspension Bridge was opened to foot travel on December 1, 1866. It stood as a testimony to the regional relationship between Ohio and Kentucky that superseded the national rift between North and South.

When the bridge was built, it was the longest suspension bridge in the world and the first to use both vertical suspenders and diagonal stays fanning from either tower. What enabled Roebling to create this wonder were some of his previous patents on wire rope, which he then found a way to spin into heavy iron wire cables right on site. He also developed a simple way to anchor these cables. All of these concepts were revolutionary; without them, neither Cincinnati's nor the Brooklyn Bridge would exist.

Roebling sustained a foot injury while working on the Brooklyn Bridge and developed tetanus. He died shortly after the Brooklyn Bridge was begun, so the work fell to his son, Washington A. Roebling.

During the flood of 1937, the Roebling Suspension Bridge was the only bridge still above water, because it had been built high enough for the steamboats' stacks to pass safely below it.

In 1984, the bridge was officially renamed the John A. Roebling Suspension Bridge, but most Cincinnatians still call it just "the Suspension Bridge."

NATIONAL UNDERGROUND RAILROAD FREEDOM CENTER

Modern readers of Harriet Beecher Stowe's *Uncle Tom's Cabin* and Toni Morrison's *Beloved* might wonder how fleeing slaves could cross such a deep, fast river as the Ohio. It was not as deep then as it is today, but to a non-swimmer back then, the Ohio was no doubt terrifying regardless of the depth.

Many slaves braved the Ohio River, deep or not, because slavery was illegal in Ohio, right from the very start. The Northwest Ordinance of 1787, which brought John Cleves Symmes and his party to Ohio in the first place, forbade involuntary servitude except as punishment for a crime. Nevertheless, many white southerners were surprised when they moved into Ohio, expecting to keep "their" slaves.

Ohioans were torn. Starting in 1807, the state legislature began passing a series of "Black Laws," making it increasingly difficult for free people of color to settle in the state. Every black person was required to pay a bond of $1,500 as a guarantee of good behavior. No person of color could testify in court against a white person. Black people were prevented from entering public institutions such as schools, hospitals, the asylum and the poorhouse.

As would be the case a hundred years later during the civil rights movement, the African American community itself was torn. Some people started petitions to have the Black Laws repealed. Some people of color (like artist Robert Duncanson) fled farther north into Canada. Some stayed to fight for their homes. As Alvin Harlow put it in his 1950 book, *The Serene Cincinnatians*:

> *Nowhere else in our history has there been a city situated quite as was Cincinnati in those years; a city on free soil, yet just across a narrow river from slavery and deriving most of its essential trade from that area; a city where idealism, humanitarianism, and the New England conscience were forced into a bitter battle with self-interest; a city where Northern blood predominated in the greater concerns of business and industry, but whose very life seemed to depend upon maintenance of friendship with the slave-holding South by tacit condonation of its chief sin.*[81]

Cincinnati occupied a strange position as the Civil War approached—politically, geographically and emotionally. It did business with both the North and the South. Cincinnati's large German population tended to support the fledgling Republican Party, while the city's largest newspaper—the *Cincinnati Daily Enquirer*—supported the South and the Democrats. Despite its now-famous stations on the Underground Railroad and strong abolitionist voices, such as those of Salmon P. Chase, Levi Coffin and Lyman Beecher, Cincinnati was home to just as many people who supported slavery. In the *Journal of Southern History*, Charles R. Wilson, in his article "Cincinnati's Reputation During the Civil War," said, "Cincinnati's slogan from 1861 to 1865 might well have been 'Peace—with the Constitution as it is, the Union as it was, and the negroes where they are.'"

Overall, Cincinnati seemed to just prefer the status quo. Nevertheless, Ohio supported the war, with Ohioans fighting in every major battle—wearing the blue *and* the gray. Several Civil War generals came from Ohio, including Ulysses S. Grant (whose horse was named Cincinnati), Rutherford B. Hayes (who became president of the United States), William H. Lytle

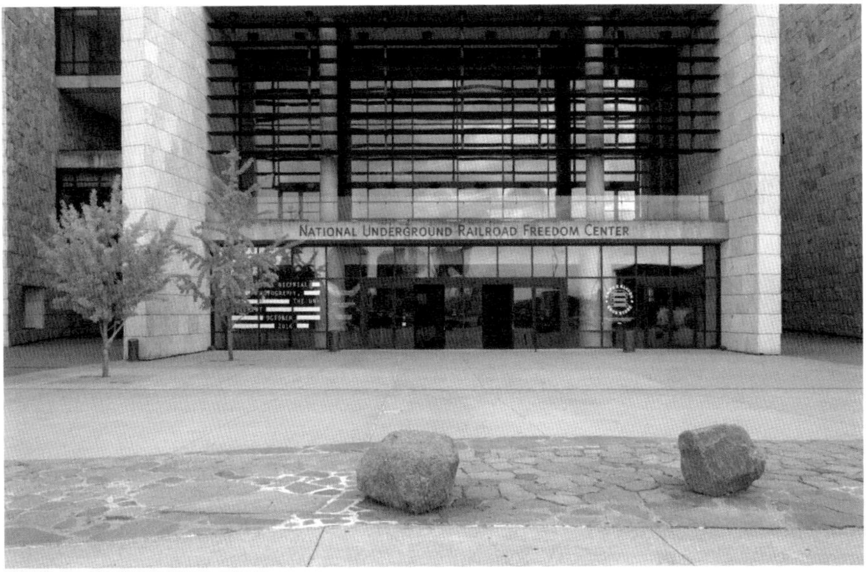

The National Underground Railroad Freedom Center was established in 2004 near the banks of the Ohio River in downtown Cincinnati. *Carol M. Highsmith, Library of Congress.*

(who was killed in action), Ormsby M. Mitchel (who founded the Cincinnati Observatory), George A. Custer (who later died in the Battle of Little Bighorn), William T. Sherman (known for burning his way to the Atlantic) and Charles Clark (born in Cincinnati, became a Confederate general and later governor of Mississippi).

So here was Cincinnati's position: it faced the South. It depended economically on northern Kentucky. Kentucky was a slaveholding state; Ohio was not. Cincinnati was a mix of abolitionists, slave owners, Underground Railroad conductors, freemen, former slaves and slave hunters. And now it houses the National Underground Railroad Freedom Center.[82]

The Underground Railroad was neither underground nor a railroad. It was a series of homes, locations and people who were willing to risk their lives to save those of others. "Conductors" on the Underground Railroad were both black and white, both male and female. Many homes in Cincinnati still have secret rooms or passageways, hangovers from a painful time.

The National Underground Railroad Freedom Center opened in 2004 on Second Street, in an area now known as "the Banks." Through a combination of permanent displays and temporary exhibits, the Freedom Center educates visitors and enables them to experience in a small way what the thousands of escaping slaves endured. One of the most chilling exhibits is a slave pen from the early 1800s, in which slaves were held while waiting to be sold. Exhibits are not limited to the American experience but also shed a light on human relations around the world. One visit to the National Underground Railroad Freedom Center is not enough. Learn before you go at www.freedomcenter.org.

Spring Grove Cemetery and Arboretum

The Spring Grove Cemetery and Arboretum is not your grandmother's cemetery. Or is it?

Spring Grove Cemetery began as a response to the cholera epidemics in the early 1800s. The small church cemeteries where people were buried were getting too full and could not properly inter the deceased. Because of a lack of knowledge about cholera and fear of infection, a new site out of town was preferred. Just like Goldilocks, the new cemetery had to be not too far, but not too close.

The Cincinnati Horticultural Society formed a Cemetery Association in 1844 and traveled the United States and Europe to get ideas for its new cemetery. A beautiful site with rolling hills was found in the northern suburb off Winton Avenue. On December 1, 1844, Salmon P. Chase drew up the Articles of Incorporation (and is also one of the justices of the Supreme Court buried there). A special act allowed the cemetery to become a nonprofit nondenominational corporation, with the first burial on September 1, 1845.[83] The "lawn plan" developed by Adolph Strauch came to be the universal standard for cemeteries. By 1850, Spring Grove boasted 4,300 ornamental plant varieties with 11,300 nursery plants in stock.

"Residents" of Spring Grove Cemetery range from everyday neighbors and friends to Supreme Court justices and war heroes. Veterans buried in Spring Grove include heroes from the Revolutionary War and the Civil War—both sides. Poet and Civil War brigadier general William Haines Lytle was buried in Spring Grove after his body was brought back to Ohio from Georgia. Other familiar names include William Goforth, James Kemper, John Ludlow, Judge Jacob Burnet and Andrew Erkenbrecher.

In 1987, the name was officially changed to the Spring Grove Cemetery and Arboretum. It is the second-largest cemetery in the country and is one of only seven cemeteries designated as a National Historic Landmark. Of its 733 acres, only 450 are developed with maintained landscaping.[84]

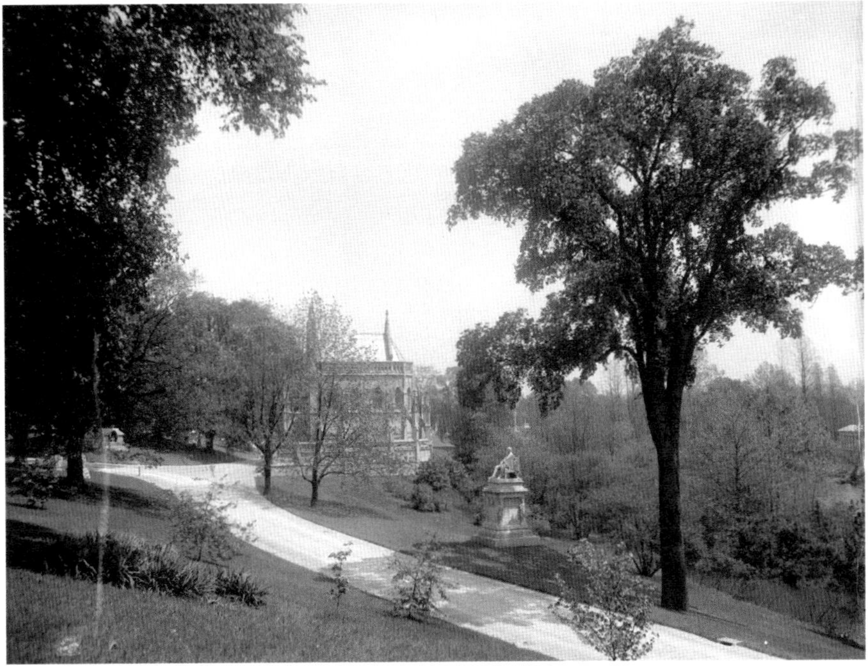

Spring Grove Cemetery and Arboretum holds a treasure of historical and horticultural gems. *Library of Congress.*

Many Cincinnatians appreciate the Spring Grove Cemetery and Arboretum for its beauty and its eclectic assortment of trees. It is one of only two cemeteries deemed a Level III Accredited site by the Morton Arboretum Register. The cemetery offers a venue for wedding photos—or even the wedding itself! Visitors can walk the grounds or ride along the winding roads by bike or automobile. Spring Grove also offers regular guided tours focusing on different aspects of the cemetery and grounds. Maps are available at the main gate for self-guided tours.[85] For more information about the Spring Grove Cemetery and Arboretum, visit www.springgrove.org.

GEORGE REMUS

George Remus was a true jack-of-all-trades: he was an optometrist, store clerk, pharmacist, lawyer, bootlegger—and convicted felon. Remus was born in 1876 in Germany and, with his parents, immigrated to the United

States when he was four. He became a successful Chicago criminal defense attorney before coming to Cincinnati and becoming what some called the "King of the Bootleggers." Many believe that he was the inspiration for F. Scott Fitzgerald's character Jay Gatsby. Indeed, Fitzgerald and Remus had met at the Seelbach Hotel in Louisville.

Young George was only fourteen when his father became incapacitated, so he had to become the man of the house quickly. He quit school and went to work for his uncle as a drugstore clerk. While working for his uncle, Remus also attended pharmacy school and became a licensed pharmacist at nineteen. Two years later, he bought his uncle's drugstore. He received his optometry license. Not satisfied, he started studying law in night school. By 1900, he had passed the Illinois bar. He was twenty-four. Remus broke ground for the use of the temporary insanity plea. That played a role in his later life. In today's dollars, Remus was pulling in the equivalent of half a million a year as a defense attorney.

The Volstead Act was passed by Congress to become the Eighteenth Amendment and, despite President Woodrow Wilson's veto, was passed on October 20, 1919. Therefore, Prohibition went into effect in January 1920. Soon, most of Remus's clients were bootleggers. At some point, Remus's entrepreneurial spirit kicked in, and he realized that he could make even more money as a bootlegger himself.

When Prohibition took effect (1920–33), not all alcohol was illegal. The Eighteenth Amendment to the U.S. Constitution merely prohibited the manufacture, transportation and sale of "intoxicating liquors." Drinking in one's own home or selling or possessing alcohol for medicinal, scientific or industrial purposes was not illegal.

Enter Remus the pharmacist. At the time Prohibition hit, millions of gallons of alcohol sat in warehouses and private holdings. Remus aimed to get his hands on that alcohol. Not only was he a legitimate pharmacist, but he also owned a number of wholesale drug companies, perfect for the dispensing of his "medicinal" alcohol.

The Chicago scene was too crowded with bootleggers, so Remus moved to Cincinnati in 1920. He bought Henry Lackman's mansion on Hermosa Avenue, calling it the "Marble Palace." (Henry's father, Herman, had opened Herman Lackman Brewing Company in 1890; it was open for twenty-nine years before it got snagged by Prohibition.)[86]

Much of the alcohol that George Remus coveted was stored in Cincinnati's factories and warehouses. He established his own distillery, obtained the appropriate documents from cronies in Washington, D.C., and set up shop.

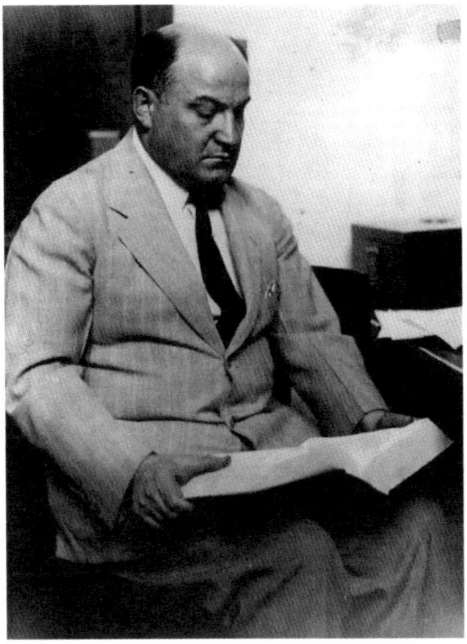

Chicago lawyer and Cincinnati bootlegger George Remus. *Library of Congress.*

As far as his income went, Remus made the right decision. In 1921, he made the equivalent of $33 million—in only three months.

Besides the Marble Palace in Price Hill, Remus also owned a roaming, hilly estate nicknamed Death Valley Ranch in Westwood, along Queen City Avenue. It was a perfect location: with its hills, he could position a lookout at the entrance to the long drive. Remus bought the farm from John Gehrum, who became one of his best defenders. Gehrum's name can be seen on a very short street off Queen City, where the Ranch had been, what is now Aspen Village Apartments. It is believed to be the only illegal distillery in Cincinnati that was never successfully raided.

Finally, though, the law caught up with him. Remus thought that because he had so many politicians, federal marshals and even a Justice Department official in his pocket he was safe from the law. This was not the case. When he was arrested in 1921, Remus controlled liquor sales in nine states and had three-thousand-plus employees working around the clock in his factories. He was charged with three thousand counts of illegally distributing alcohol and was found guilty. He appealed all the way up to the Supreme Court but lost and had to go to prison. While he was in prison, he gave control over everything to his wife, Imogene, including his power of attorney. He also became friendly with another inmate, who turned out to be an undercover prohibition agent who was there undercover on another case.

One of his ten distilleries was the former Fleischmann Distillery, which he had bought for $197,000. While Remus was in prison for bootlegging, he asked Imogene to contact Franklin Dodge, the federal agent who helped put him there, to expedite his release. Evidently, Imogene had something else on her mind, because she began to have an affair with Dodge. Then bit by bit, she began selling off Remus's belongings, including the Fleischmann Distillery, which she sold for $18,000—of which she sent Remus $100.

Imogene and Dodge had a grand old time in Remus's mansion, which she stripped almost bare—leaving a gun in the garage. While Remus was in prison, his wife first tried to divorce him, then have him deported and then have him killed. When Remus got out of prison, he sought out Imogene right away and ran her down with his car. As she tried to flee, Remus shot and killed her with the gun she had left in the garage. He killed Imogene on October 6, 1927—the day their divorce went into effect.

Remus decided to represent himself at trial; his plea was "not guilty by reason of insanity," which he is credited with creating. Prosecuting the case was thirty-year-old Charles Phelps Taft II, son of chief justice of the United States and former president William Howard Taft. After less than twenty minutes of deliberation, the jury found Remus not guilty by reason of insanity. He spent two months in the state hospital for the criminally insane. He then appealed his insanity successfully, so he was able to leave—a free man.

Remus married his third wife, Covington's Blanche Watson. He sold real estate and bought stock in the Reds. He spent most of the rest of his life trying to recover all the assets that Imogene had stolen or sold. He died in 1952 and is buried in Blanche's family plot in Falmouth, Kentucky. The ironic thing in all this is that Remus was a teetotaler.

Cincinnati Museum Center

Union Terminal is the home of the Cincinnati Museum Center (CMC). Construction started in 1986, with the doors opening in 1990. CMC houses multiple museums that were previously scattered around the city: the Museum

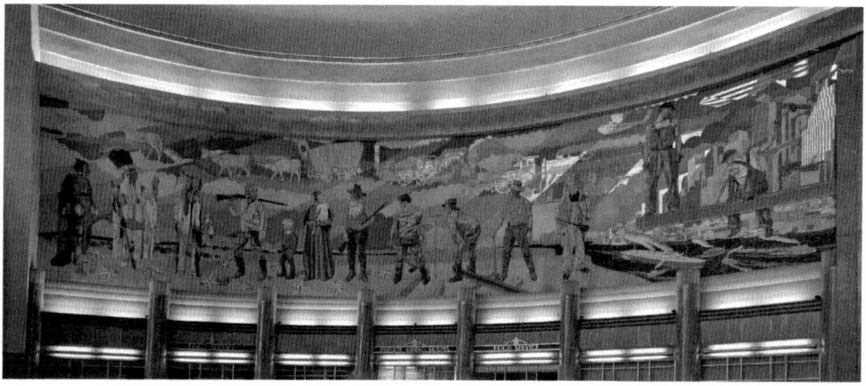

One of four murals from the Cincinnati Museum Center. *Carol M. Highsmith, Library of Congress.*

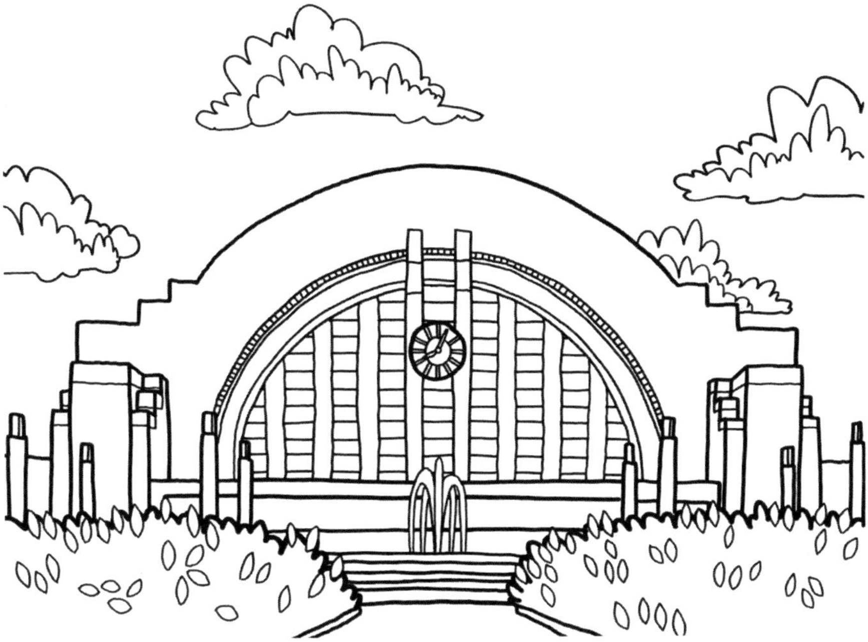

Cincinnati Museum Center is three museums in one: Cincinnati History Museum, Museum of Natural History and Science and the Cinergy Children's Museum. *Illustration by Allison Ranieri.*

of Natural History and Science, the Cincinnati History Museum and the Cincinnati History Library and Archives. The Cincinnati History Library and Archives is a treasure-trove of historic documents and photographs.

After the flood of 1997 wreaked havoc on the Children's Museum in Longworth Hall, the Duke Energy Children's Museum opened in the Cincinnati Museum Center. CMC has a strong educational focus. Since 1989, CMC has been encouraging youth (ages thirteen and above) to volunteer through the CMC Youth Program.

Besides the exhibits, CMC also offers programs on history, culture and science. It is also the site of the Richard D. Lindner Family OMNIMAX Theater. The five-story, 260-degree domed theater makes moviegoers truly part of the experience. For more information and exhibit schedules, visit www.cincymuseum.org.

CHAPTER 8
PEOPLE

TAFTS

At the end of the 1830s, New Englander Alphonso Taft made an exploratory trip from his native Vermont out west after earning his law degree from Yale College. Taft settled in Cincinnati, got a job as an apprentice at a law office and sat for the Ohio bar exam. Upon passing the bar, Taft set up his law practice. Taft married fellow Vermonter Fanny Phelps in 1841 and became active in the First Congregational Church (Unitarian). He had been brought up a Baptist and had attended a few of Lyman Beecher's services at the Second Presbyterian Church. However, he felt the First Congregational Church to be most welcoming. He and Fanny became members. Together they had five children, but only two survived childhood. Fanny died from tuberculosis in 1852, at which time Alphonso's parents came from New England to live with him and to help with the two surviving boys: Charles Phelps and Peter Rawson Taft.

Taft married again the following year, this time to a Massachusetts woman named Louisa Maria "Louise" Torrey. Together they had five more children: four boys and a girl. The first son, Samuel, died of pertussis at fourteen months. The second son was William Howard Taft, who would one day become president of the United States. Of Alphonso's ten children, the first died in 1848 and the youngest died in 1950—102 years apart.

By 1873, Judge Alphonso Taft was through with his service to Ohio's Superior Court. He established a law firm—A. Taft and Sons, Attorneys at Law—and was joined by eldest sons Charles Phelps and Peter Rawson Taft. All but one of his sons became attorneys and practiced law. Those four graduated from the University of Cincinnati College of Law. Horace, instead, founded the Taft School for Boys in Watertown, Connecticut.

William Howard Taft is today the most famous Taft, having served as both president and chief justice of the United States. William Howard Taft said that sitting on the Supreme Court was his life's most meaningful accomplishment. He did not enjoy being president, and when he was unhappy, he ate. That is probably why he is known nationally as the president who once got stuck in a bathtub and had a bathtub large enough for four grown men in the White House. No definitive proof exists of Taft's bathtub predicament. However, in Ike Hoover's book *42 Years in the White House*, Hoover stated that the unfortunate incident had, indeed, occurred. As Hoover had been chief White House usher during Taft's presidency, this probably confirms it.

Former president William Howard Taft was appointed by a fellow Ohioan, President Warren G. Harding, chief justice of the United States in 1921. President Theodore Roosevelt had offered Taft a Supreme Court appointment many times previously, but Taft had always refused. At the time, Taft had been civil governor of Cuba and was heavily involved in developments in the Philippines.

But when the chief justice position was left vacant by the death of Edward Douglass White, Taft eagerly accepted the offer. Ironically, by accepting the Supreme Court appointment, he replaced a man whom he had appointed. (He was also succeeded as chief justice by another of his appointments.) As chief justice of the United States, William Howard Taft administered the oath of office to Presidents Calvin Coolidge and Woodrow Wilson. He was the only former president to ever do so.

Thirty-four years after Alphonso Taft's death, the University of Cincinnati dedicated its new Alphonso Taft College of Law building on October 28, 1925. In attendance were the four surviving Taft brothers, from eldest to youngest: Charles Phelps Taft, William Howard Taft, Henry Waters Taft and Horace Dutton Taft. (Peter Rawson Taft II, named after Alphonso's father, survived infancy but died two years before Alphonso.)

When someone sent William Howard Taft a photograph of the event, he responded with a letter in which he wrote, "I note your enclosure of the photograph of my three brothers and myself. There is a good deal of

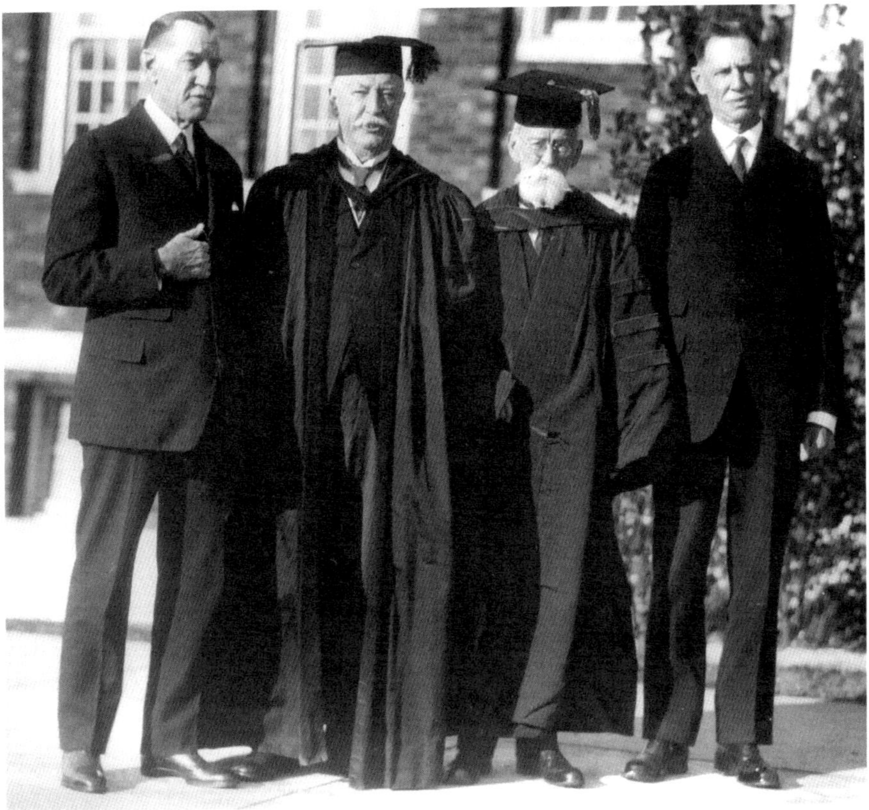

Left to right: Henry Waters Taft, Chief Justice William Howard Taft, Charles Phelps Taft and Horace Dutton Taft. *Archives & Rare Books Library, University of Cincinnati.*

avoirdupois [extra weight] and length in that group. It was a family meeting in Cincinnati where we met to take part in the dedication of a new building called the Alphonso Taft Hall, for the housing of the Law School of the University of Cincinnati, and it is a great pleasure to have secured a photograph of this kind."

At the time, Henry was a lawyer, Charles was publisher of the *Cincinnati Times-Star* and Horace was headmaster of the Taft School for Boys in Connecticut. William, of course, was a former president and the existing chief justice of the United States. William Howard Taft served on the Supreme Court until just a month before his death in March 1930.

As the twentieth century dawned, the Taft family continued to lead the way in Ohio and national politics. William Howard Taft's eldest son, Robert A. Taft, desperately wanted to follow in his father's footsteps. He had graduated first in his classes at Yale and Harvard Law and was at the top of those passing the Ohio bar in 1913. With his brother, Charles, he established the Cincinnati law firm of Taft, Stettinius & Hollister.

Although Robert A. Taft held many public offices in both Ohio and Washington, he was never able to reach the Oval Office. He was, however, the first son of a president since John Quincy Adams to serve in Congress. Robert Taft was well liked on both sides of the aisle but could not gain enough support from fellow Republicans. In August 1941, he voted against extending the draft. Then on December 6, 1941, he was overheard asking why an armed force of two million men was necessary. The next morning proved why it was necessary when the Empire of Japan bombed the U.S. naval base at Pearl Harbor.

Robert Taft became President Dwight Eisenhower's trusted confidant in Congress in the 1950s, but this relationship was cut short by Taft's failing health. Four months after experiencing pain while golfing with the president, Taft died from advanced, inoperable cancer in July 1953. He was only sixty-three years old. His son, Robert Taft Jr., followed in his father's political footsteps, serving four terms as a state senator and three in Washington. He, too, was ultimately defeated and chose to return to the family law firm.

William Howard Taft's younger son, Charles Phelps Taft II, was no slacker. He helped create a new city charter and form of government in Cincinnati to break the Republican hold on the city. He was elected Hamilton County prosecutor in 1926, followed by a city council seat in 1937. During World War II, "Charlie" Taft served in the Roosevelt administration in several capacities, earning him the nickname "New Deal Republican." He remained in Cincinnati City Hall until he retired in 1977 at the age of eighty. He died in June 1983 and is buried in Spring Grove Cemetery in the Taft family plot.

Robert A. "Bob" Taft III, great-grandson of William Howard Taft, entered the family business of holding public office, serving as a state legislator, Hamilton County commissioner, Ohio secretary of state and governor. His daughter, Anna, has not pursued public office but instead has dedicated herself to public service of another sort. In 2006, she created the nonprofit Tandana Foundation, a cross-cultural volunteer program that provides scholarships and funding for small community projects and healthcare volunteer mission trips in Ecuador and Mali's Dogon Country, in sub-Saharan Africa. (*Tandana* means "to gather together" or "to unite" in Kichwa, an indigenous language of the Andes.) Both Bob Taft and former Ohio first lady Hope Taft are very supportive of their daughter's work and in carrying out its missions.[87]

LAZARUSES? LAZARI?

When the name on the Shillito's department stores started changing, many longtime Cincinnatians cringed. John Shillito, one of the founding fathers of Cincinnati, established his store in 1830. From 1830 to 1982, the department stores bore his name. However, in 1928—long before the names started changing—the F. & R. (named for sons Fred and Ralph) Lazarus Company bought the John Shillito Company.

Why? Part of the reason was business: Shillito's had slid from its proud past as king of the Queen City and had fallen to fourth place in sales in the Cincinnati retail market. Another reason was sentimentality: Fred and Ralph's mother, Amelia, had grown up in Cincinnati and had bought her trousseau at Shillito's.

In 1929, Columbus-based F. & R. Lazarus joined forces with New York's Abraham & Straus and Bloomingdale's and Filene's of Boston to create Federated Department Stores, right before the stock market crash of 1929. When Fred Lazarus Jr., grandson of patriarch Simon Lazarus, became chairman of Federated in 1945, he moved the company headquarters to Cincinnati. In the words of Humphrey Bogart in *Casablanca*, it was the beginning of a beautiful friendship between the Lazarus family and the people of Cincinnati.

Lazarus had long been known in Columbus as a family- and community-oriented company. In Cincinnati, it was no different. It moved to the city and hit the ground running. And driving—Fred Lazarus Jr. was one of the forces behind the construction of I-75.

One of the things that shoppers and cooks can thank Fred Lazarus Jr. for is having Thanksgiving forever fixed as the third Thursday of November. To give retailers a longer shopping season before Christmas, Lazarus managed to convince President Franklin to buck the presidential trend and in 1939 made the change. Well, calendar makers, schools and football players weren't too happy about the confusion. It took an act of Congress in 1941 to settle on the third Thursday for good.

Fred Jr.'s son Ralph co-founded the Cincinnati Business Committee. Ralph's brother Simon became president of the Cincinnati Bar Association and a longtime legal advocate for the poor, including being president of the Legal Aid Society. Simon was also one of the original authors of the Civil Rights Act. As great as the works of the sons were, however, their good deeds pale in the face of Simon's grandson Fred III and his wife, Irma.

Irma was a *tour de force* in the Cincinnati philanthropic scene. She founded the Ohio Arts Council and—with her husband—was a fierce supporter of the Fine Arts Fund (now ArtsWave), as well as many of its charter beneficiaries, such as the Cincinnati Symphony and the Cincinnati Ballet, serving on the boards of several. For thirty-five years, she hosted a show, *Conversations with Irma*, on WCET, Cincinnati's public television station and one of the oldest in the country. Irma used this show as a platform to raise awareness of AIDS and support for research and its victims—way before it was "cool" to do so. In 1993, she was awarded the Ohio Arts Council's Governor's Award for half a century of leadership in the arts.

Up in Columbus, Robert Jr., the last Lazarus family member in Federated Department Stores, handed over the reins in 2002 and died in December 2013. The other "Lazari" have left retail, and many have left the area, but they have not left the family tradition of community service. They left something else behind, too: lizards.

There are no Lazarus lizards in Columbus. There are plenty in Cincinnati, though—especially on the east side. Sadly, though, most of the family responsible for their presence is long gone. But we in Cincinnati have many more positive memories of the Lazarus family than a bunch of reptiles.

So, what *about* those lizards? In a way, we have Irma to thank for those. In 1934, she had married George Rau and moved to his native Switzerland. However, as the rumblings of World War II began, because she was Jewish Irma felt Switzerland was unsafe. She divorced Rau and returned to the United States in 1939, along with her two children. In 1941, she married Fred Lazarus III.

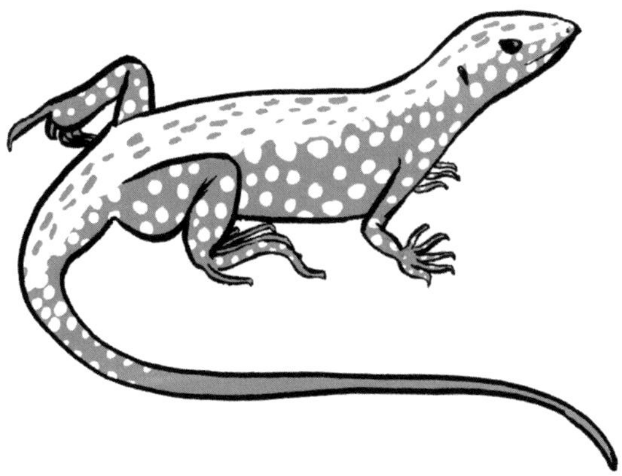

The Lazarus family is famous in Ohio for its chain of department stores and in Cincinnati for the "Lazarus lizards." *Illustration by Allison Ranieri.*

Now, according to her son George's own words, in a letter he wrote to researchers at the University of Cincinnati, in 1951 he snuck about ten lizards in a sock (kids, please don't do this) home from vacation in northern Italy near the Lago di Garda. Luckily for the little reptiles, as George wrote, "the climate in that section of Italy is almost exactly the same as Cincinnati, and they thrived upon my letting them go at my home on Torrence Court." The invasive *Podarcis muralis* or "wall lizard" became so indigenous that it is now counted by many as a local species. An aggressive thing, it often crowds out the local guys.

So after a long, dedicated tradition with the folks of Cincinnati, when we roll the stone away, the only Lazarus we might find is a wall lizard scurrying for cover.[88]

A Store by Any Other Name…

Shillito's	1830–1982
Shillito-Rike's	1982–1986
Lazarus	1986–2003
Lazarus-Macy's	2003–2005
Macy's	2005–present

DeHart Hubbard

William DeHart Hubbard was born on November 25, 1903, the eldest of William and Carrie Hubbard's eight children. "DeHart" grew up fast and strong, attending Douglass School and then Walnut Hills High School, where he excelled in academics and athletics. If he had lived in the twenty-first century, he would be a prime candidate for college. However, back then, with opportunities for African Americans limited, his future was not so clear.

DeHart Hubbard caught the attention of University of Michigan alumnus Lon Barringer. Barringer, a resident of West Virginia, had followed the high school career of young DeHart in the Cincinnati newspapers. Barringer felt the young man's strong athletic and academic prowess he had exhibited at Walnut Hills High School would be a good fit for the University of Michigan. However, Barringer knew that head football coach and fellow West Virginian Fielding Yost had blocked other African Americans from playing for Michigan. He also knew that Yost had just been named Michigan's athletic director and would be looking out for the success of the school's athletes.

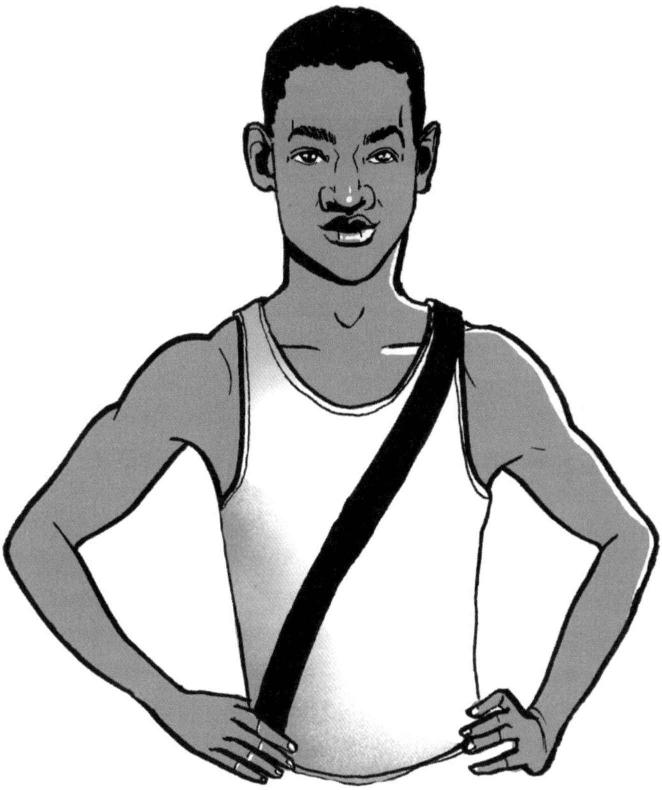

DeHart Hubbard was the first African American to win an individual gold medal at the Olympics. *Illustration by Allison Ranieri.*

Fortunately for Michigan and Hubbard, the *Cincinnati Enquirer* was holding a contest to increase its subscription base and to help local high school students. The ten students who brought in the most new subscriptions would earn $3,000 scholarships to the colleges of their choice. In a very unorthodox move, Barringer convinced DeHart to enter the contest, assuring him that he would do everything he could to help. Barringer sent a letter to all of DeHart's Cincinnati supporters and to almost every Michigan alum in the country. New subscriptions poured in. As a result, Hubbard enrolled at the University of Michigan in September 1921.

Hubbard excelled at Michigan, participating in track and field. As a freshman, he was unable to participate in varsity events, but he was allowed to participate in an AAU event in New Jersey. His success at that event qualified him for the 1924 Paris Olympics (the setting for the movie *Chariots of Fire*). As an African American, he was not allowed to participate in all the events for which he qualified, but he was allowed to do the long jump. He won the gold medal—the first African American from the United States to win an individual Olympic gold medal, twelve years before Jesse Owens.

Hubbard returned to America and the University of Michigan, where the following year he set a world record (25 feet, 10¾ inches) for the long jump. In 1926, he tied the world record (9.6 seconds) for the 100-yard dash. DeHart Hubbard graduated with honors from the University of Michigan in 1927 as a three-time track-and-field NCAA All-American and seven-time track-and-field Big Ten Conference champion. Upon graduation, he went to work for the Cincinnati Public Recreation Commission and later the Federal Public Housing Authority in Cleveland. His athletic abilities and commitment to public service were later reflected in his great-nephew, one-time Cincinnati mayor and Ohio secretary of state J. Kenneth Blackwell.[89]

NEIL ARMSTRONG

The country knows Neil Armstrong as the first man to walk on the moon on July 20, 1969. Most of us of a certain age can easily recall the crackled message of "It's one small step for man, one giant leap for mankind." With these words, the blurry figure stepped from the capsule onto the barren, pocked lunar surface. (Armstrong said later that the transmission edited his words. He swore that he meant to say, "One small step for *a* man..." He

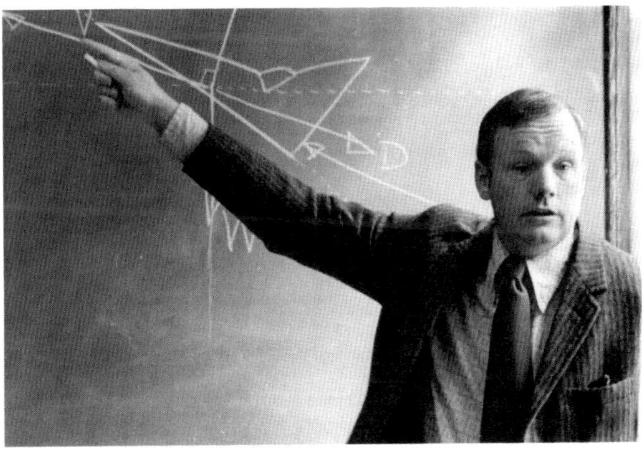

Ohio astronaut Neil Armstrong served on faculty in the UC Aerospace Engineering Department, the second-oldest such department in the country. *Library of Congress.*

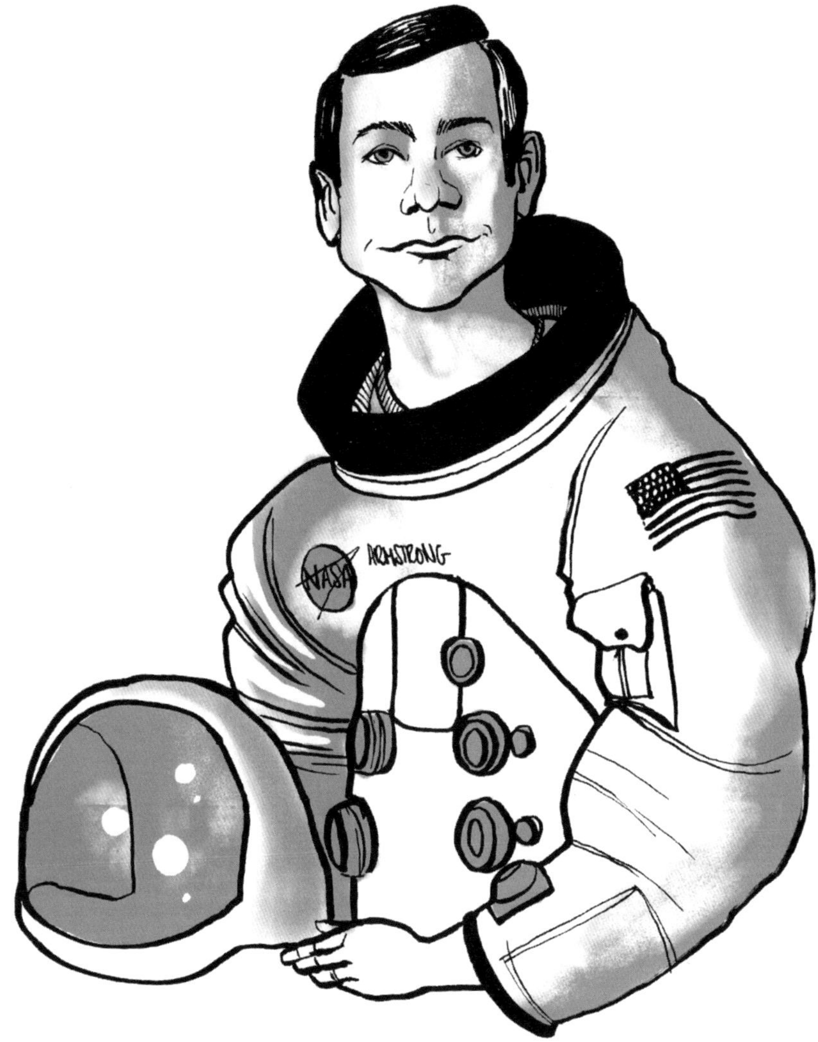

Neil Armstrong was the first human to walk on the moon. *Illustration by Allison Ranieri.*

didn't want to imply any assumption of gender in his statement.) I'm sure I was not the only person who stepped outside to see if the moon looked different. Try as I might, however, my eleven-year-old eyes couldn't pick out any capsule or footprints.

As Armstrong bounced around in the lower gravity, he looked something like the Michelin Man or Mister Stay Puft Man. Somewhat less famous than his statement as he stepped onto the moon's surface is what he sang while bouncing around on the moon's surface: "Hippity hoppity, hippity hoppity, over hill...."

Before his famous steps, Armstrong was already a hero. He had served as a naval aviator in the Korean War. As the pilot of the Gemini 8 mission, he was the first person to successfully dock two vehicles in space in 1966.[90]

People of Cincinnati knew Armstrong to be a quiet man and intensely private. He was dismayed when his barber kept some hair clippings and tried to sell them. Some people in Cincinnati knew Armstrong as something else: *Professor* Armstrong. From 1971 to 1979, he served on the faculty of the University of Cincinnati's Aerospace Engineering Department. UC's aerospace program was accustomed to celebrity: it had been designed in 1929 by aviation pioneer Bradley Jones, consulting with Orville Wright. Jones designed the instrumentation that pilots rely on, and it was this instrumentation that Charles Lindbergh had insisted on for his historic transatlantic flight. It is no wonder that Ohio is referred to as the "birthplace of aviation." UC's is the second-oldest aerospace program in the country and the first to be chaired by a woman. Armstrong had received his own degrees in aerospace engineering from Purdue University and the University of Southern California.

Still, despite his shying away from "star status," Armstrong popped up in surprising places. At the Riverbend Music Center in 1984 and again in 2009, he narrated Aaron Copland's "Lincoln Portrait" for his friend Erich Kunzel, director of the Cincinnati Pops Orchestra. As discussed elsewhere in this book, Copland's piece had been commissioned by the Cincinnati Symphony Orchestra. How fitting, then, that one of the most memorable performances was Armstrong with the Cincinnati Pops.

Armstrong died on August 25, 2012; his cremated remains were buried at sea on September 14, 2012, in the Atlantic Ocean.

MARY EMERY

One of those who came from Europe to take advantage of Porkopolis was Thomas Emery. Born in England, he immigrated to the United States in 1832 with his wife and his son, Thomas Josephus Emery. Emery did not always enjoy success making candles. Upon arrival from England, he tried a number of ventures that didn't pan out. His first attempts only landed him in bankruptcy. He attempted to raise silkworms in Kentucky, but the mulberry trees kept dying and so did the silkworms. He crossed the river to Cincinnati and dabbled in real estate, but he bought more land than he sold. Finally, he got on the Porkopolis bandwagon and turned to what we now know as oleochemicals. Emery began dabbling in soaps and lard oil. Soon enough, Thomas Emery had found his niche: real estate and fatty acids.

He founded the Lard Oil Company in 1840 (later changing the name to Emery Candle Company). His sons Thomas J. and John Josiah joined him in the business. Emery's business boomed by the mid-1840s, but he didn't live long past that to enjoy it. He fell through a hatch in his own factory and died in 1857. The trustees of his estate soon recognized that Emery's eldest two sons, Thomas Josephus and John Josiah—then in their twenties—were better suited to run their father's business than they were. (Emery had also had another son, J. Howard, and two daughters, Julia and Kezia, but they didn't take an active role in the business as did Thomas and John.)

By the 1880s, in addition to Thomas Emery's lard oil factory, the property management side of their father's business was flourishing under the Emery sons' hands. Thomas Emery's Sons, Incorporated (which became Emery Industries, Inc., in 1928 and was much later merged into National Distillers), built hotels, apartment houses and business buildings all over Cincinnati. Tom, the elder brother, felt that some of the other hotels in town were profiting too much off their guests and offered rates about 50 percent below those of the best hotels, such as the Burnet and the Grand. The Emerys built the Palace Hotel in 1882 and charged two dollars a day for room and board.

Thomas J. Emery married Mary Hopkins in 1866. Samuel Hannaford built their family home, the Edgecliffe, which overlooked the Ohio River. Sadly, theirs was not to remain a happy family for long. They had two sons: Sheldon, born in 1867, and Albert, born in 1868. Albert died at the age of sixteen as the result of a sledding accident, and Sheldon died at twenty-three from pneumonia while a student at Harvard.

When Thomas died in 1906, he left his widow a "lonely millionaire" for twenty-one years: he left her his $20 million fortune with no directives as to how to spend it.

Mary Emery (known as "Guppy" to her friends) felt she had what she called a "vast responsibility" to the people of Cincinnati and opened her purse and her heart to them. She became known as "Lady Bountiful" as she stepped in like an angel and saved the opera, the zoo, Holmes Hospital and many other organizations that were on the cusp of nonexistence. She

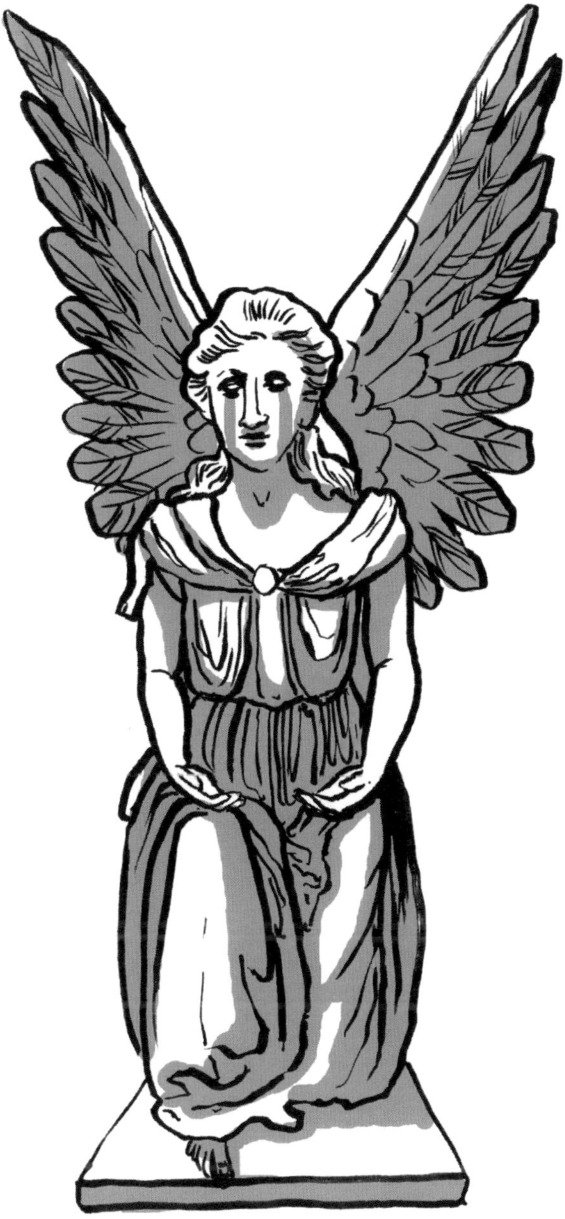

The "Emery Angel" marks the tomb of Thomas J. and Mary Emery at Spring Grove Cemetery and Arboretum. *Illustration by Allison Ranieri.*

donated an entire wing and more than $3 million worth of art from her own collection to the Cincinnati Art Museum.

Her most magnanimous gesture of largesse is probably Mariemont (pronounced MARE-ee-mont), arguably one of the first planned communities in the United States. She felt that the living conditions in downtown Cincinnati were deplorable, so she procured a large tract of land on the east side of town. Working with architect John Nolen, she endeavored to create a community with an English country garden feel. They named it after her estate in Rhode Island, which her beloved Thomas had built for her.

Mary Emery died in 1927 at the age of eighty-three. Tom and Mary Emery had no heirs; Tom's younger brother John was still a bachelor in his sixties, but he married a twenty-two-year-old woman and had five children to pass on the family name and philanthropic tradition. That tradition was carried on in John J. Emery Jr., who also enjoyed success in the hotel business, building the forty-eight-story Carew Tower (Cincinnati's tallest building at the time), the Netherland Plaza and the Terrace Plaza hotels. He also founded Cincinnati Country Day School and held leadership roles with the Boy Scouts of America and the Cincinnati Art Museum. Meanwhile, his sister Audrey showed herself for having a flair for fashion and flings. She was voted one of the ten most beautiful women in America and married into Russian nobility not once, but twice, including the Grand Duke Dmitri Pavlovich, the cousin of Nicholas, Russia's last czar.

After their father died, the Emery sons relocated the factory from (appropriately named) Water Street. They moved up Vine Street all the way to the St. Bernard neighborhood, where the plant is now. The Emery sons also followed their father's footsteps in land. They owned much downtown land and built the Emery Hotel at Fifth and Race Streets. Even more importantly, Thomas J. and John Emery followed Thomas Sr.'s example in philanthropy. Among the recipients of their generosity were Children's Hospital and the Orphan Asylum for Colored Children.

In 1926, Wendell P. Dabney—highly respected editor of the African American newspaper the *Union*—wrote about the Emery sons: "In letters of gold the name Emery should be emblazoned upon the hearts of all Cincinnatians….Their recognition of the brotherhood of man caused them to refuse donations to any cause that recognized the color line, and so their princely gifts to institutions carried with them the admission of colored people."[91]

CINCINNATI POLITICS

Cincinnati has had an interesting political history, with some curious characters leading the way.

Two brothers arrived in Cincinnati during the influx of Europeans before the Civil War: Maximilian and Charles Louis Fleischmann. The Fleischmanns were from what is now known as the Czech Republic. There, Charles had managed a Vienna distillery, where he produced spirits and baked goods.

When they arrived in Cincinnati, the Fleischmann brothers immediately set to work to continue their trade. However, they were disappointed in the quality of yeast here, so they returned to Europe for European yeast. They developed a way to make compressed yeast from a byproduct of distilling rye whiskey that had been considered waste. They also invented and patented a machine for distillation. With James Graff's financial support, they opened the Vienna Model Bakery. Their renown grew for their yeast and distillation prowess. (Bootlegger George Remus bought the Fleischmann distillery.)

Besides his forays into baking and distilling, Charles was also exceedingly successful in politics. He served two terms in the Ohio senate and was an aide to William McKinley while the latter was governor of Ohio. This affinity for politics was later shared by his son Julius.[92]

One black mark in Cincinnati's political history was the rise to power of George "Boss" Cox, starting when Cox was elected to city council in 1879 at the age of twenty-six. As with other cities' political bosses, Cox ruled the city through a web of cronies and coercion. One strong voice crying out against Cox and his gang was the *Cincinnati Post*, founded by Edward Willis Scripps. Cox stayed on council for two terms and then stepped down to "pull the strings" from his unofficial position of power.

In 1901, distiller Julius Fleischmann was elected mayor; at twenty-nine, he was the youngest to ever hold that post (up to that time and since). He had broad support from many groups: the Germans liked his liberal stance on liquor; the Protestants, Jews and Catholics liked his philanthropic donations to many charities; and many appreciated him as part-owner of the Cincinnati Reds. Julius served until 1905.

Finally, the Cox machine broke, thanks to a stirring speech made by Murray Seasongood to the Cincinnatus Association on October 9, 1923. The Cincinnatus Association was a group of about fifty young businessmen organized by Captain Victor Heinz to address municipal problems in Cincinnati.

By this time, Cox was dead, but the machine was plowing forward under the direction of his protégé, Rudolph Hynicka. Seasongood had had enough. "We have the fourth-largest per capita expenditure of any city in the country," he told the association. "What do we get for it? Nothing, absolutely nothing….I for one believe that the time has come to cut out every extra tax levy, bond issue or anything else that will give the bunch a chance to squander money. Make them produce the goods on what they have or get out."

Robert A. Taft, son of William Howard Taft, finally wrote the groundbreaking—and air-clearing—charter for the City of Cincinnati in 1924. Murray Seasongood and Taft, with others, redrafted the city charter to call for a nine-member council to replace the existing thirty-two-seat board structure, a council-appointed city manager as chief administrator, a mayor selected by his or her council colleagues and a proportional representation ballot. This charter form of government took effect in 1925 and stayed in effect until it was replaced by the "strong mayor" form in 2001.

One of the city council's shining lights started out in life as Marian Alexander. She, her twin sister, Mildred, and their brothers often struggled

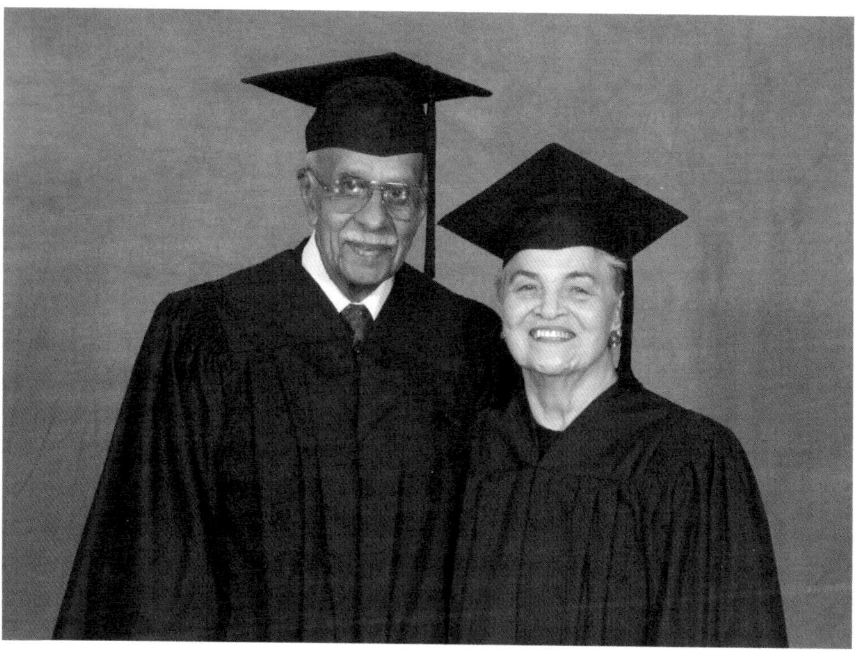

Donald and Marian Spencer received honorary degrees at the UC Spring 2006 Commencement. *University of Cincinnati Photographic Services.*

in their segregated hometown of Gallipolis, Ohio. They had to fight for the right to attend high school with white children and to be allowed into the National Honor Society. Marian joined the NAACP at the age of thirteen. In spite of (or perhaps because of) their struggle, Marian and Mildred were co-valedictorians of their high school class.

Marian and Mildred Alexander came to Cincinnati to study at the University of Cincinnati. Because African Americans were not allowed in the residence halls, the Alexander twins lived with their relatives, the Manggrums. Loretta Manggrum was their father's cousin, and William Manggrum was a pharmacist. They worked in their cousin Bill's drugstore for one whole day. That was the extent of their employment at the Manggrum Drug Store, for Bill Manggrum said that they smiled at the customers too much.

Marian's future husband, Donald Spencer, had already graduated from college and was teaching at the Douglass School when he met Marian and Mildred Alexander. Donald had formed an organization called Quadres, while still an education major, to unite people of all races and to end racial discrimination at the university. At the time, African Americans were constrained as to what colleges they were allowed in (Teachers College and Liberal Arts, for the most part), and they were not allowed to fully participate in all activities in and around campus, such as acting in the school theater productions or swimming in the YMCA pool. Not one to be dissuaded, Donald had Quadres put on its own musicals to raise money for its activities, acting in many of the productions himself. Marian had found a kindred spirit.

Donald Spencer was the first African American to become a licensed realtor in Cincinnati. Donald and Marian were married on August 28, 1940, while Marian was still a UC student. She and her sister graduated in 1942.

Besides having a smile that would light up a room (not just Manggrum's drugstore), Marian Spencer had spunk, too. In the early 1950s, Spencer heard many advertisements welcoming children to Cincinnati's Coney Island Amusement Park. When she called the amusement park to ask about the ads, she told them that she was an African American. She was then told no, actually, the ad was directed at just the white children in Cincinnati. Spencer (among others) sued Coney Island in 1952 to open its doors to African Americans. Still, the park resisted. The city finally announced in 1955 that it might not renew Coney Island's license if it did not allow African Americans in, so the park relented. However, Sunlite Pool was still restricted to whites only. Not until May 1961 was it opened to all people, regardless of color or ethnicity.

In 1975, Theodore Berry—Cincinnati's first African American mayor—appointed Marian Spencer to the University of Cincinnati Board of Trustees. She became the first African American woman elected to city council in 1983 and served as the vice mayor of Cincinnati.[93]

Marian's beloved Donald died in 2010, but she is still going strong (as of this writing) at the seasoned age of ninety-seven.

OSCAR ROBERTSON

Finding success on and off the basketball court takes hard work, a strong team, improvisation and discipline—lessons that Oscar Robertson learned early on while playing for the basketball team at Crispus Attucks High School in Indianapolis.

"The coach was strict and set up the rules," Robertson told the author in a 2009 interview. "He said, 'If you don't come to class, you're off the team. If you don't get good grades, you're off the team. If you do anything off the court to embarrass the school, you're off the team.' So I think that being involved in sports means being structured in life."

Robertson, who graduated in the top 10 percent of his high school class, carried his coach's lessons with him to UC, where he played point guard from 1957 to 1960 and led the Bearcats to the Final Four in his junior and senior seasons. He was also the first player to lead the NCAA in scoring for three consecutive seasons and win consensus player of the year honors three times.

Despite his success on the court, Robertson faced hardship of another kind outside the arena. Many times when on the road, the team stayed at hotels that didn't allow African Americans. Arrangements were made for Robertson to stay elsewhere, often in the home of a UC alumnus. Separated from his team, Robertson missed out on the communication and camaraderie that often takes place when the clock is not running. Many colleges were faced with the same dilemma in the 1960s. Some colleges, like the University of Notre Dame, refused to play any team where the integrated team could not play together. Still, "I'm not bitter," Robertson said.

After graduating from UC, Robertson took his leadership skills to the Olympics, where he co-captained the 1960 gold medal–winning basketball team with Jerry West. He was drafted by the Cincinnati Royals of the National Basketball Association (NBA), playing for the Royals from 1960 to

1970 and for the Milwaukee Bucks from 1970 to 1974. In his second NBA season, he averaged the first and only triple double (30.8 points per game, 12.5 rebounds and 11.4 assists) in NBA history before three-point shots existed. As president of the NBA Players Association (1965–74), Robertson had a lasting impact on the game by leading a class-action antitrust lawsuit against the NBA in 1970. The result changed the business of all professional sports with the 1976 "Oscar Robertson Rule," which removed restrictions on player movement imposed by the league's master agreement with its players and elevated the salaries of star athletes to those of stars in the entertainment world.

However, Robertson paid a personal price for his actions. Aside from filling in a couple of times as an interim coach for UC, he has not held a leadership role in other teams. "After I got out of basketball, I was not able to participate in basketball at all," Robertson said. Once he retired from the sport, he was "blacklisted" by NBA owners and has never been asked to coach or manage a team.

But the basketball great did not let this setback keep him from achieving business success. He simply used his well-honed leadership skills to start his own small business.

"Sometimes in life, you have to evolve," Robertson said. After initial forays into construction, real estate development and banking, he has found his niche in small, carefully chosen businesses. For example, Orchem Corporation is a leader in the "green" movement and in the fight against infectious diseases. It's also the leading minority-owned specialty chemicals manufacturer in the United States.

"I first got involved because in high school, kids were playing on football fields that were infested with disease," he explained. "Especially in fields with artificial turf, the infection never goes away, and the schools don't want to take responsibility if a kid gets hurt playing football. I got involved in this company because I wanted to make sure they neutralize the fields."

Orchem garnered national attention for its introduction of Spectrum 24, a broad-spectrum antimicrobial, antifungal and antiviral disinfectant that can provide up to twenty-four-hour residual effectiveness. Altogether, the company serves many industries: food and beverage processing sanitation (including craft breweries), general industrial cleaning, hospitality and animal care. But Robertson is modest about his company's achievements, having learned through trial and error that success does not happen overnight. "We're not setting the world on fire because it's very difficult to do," he said. "But we're holding our own."

Robertson is a frequent presence on the court at UC's home games. In 1994, a nine-foot bronze statue of Robertson was installed outside Fifth/Third Arena at UC. (It was moved in 2006 to Richard E. Lindner Varsity Village.) In September 2009, Robertson was inducted into the International Basketball Federation Hall of Fame in Madrid.[94]

RUTH LYONS AND THE RUTH LYONS CHILDREN'S FUND

You might call Cincinnati the birthplace of talk shows. The confluence of two great forces created the genre that opened the door for personalities like Oprah Winfrey, Phil Donahue, David Letterman—even Chris Hardwick on *The Talking Dead*. Those two forces? Ruth Lyons and WLW (the World's Largest Wireless).

Cincinnati entrepreneur and inventor Powel Crosley Jr. began broadcasting in July 1921 by playing his own collection of LPs from his home under the call signal of 8CR with all the power of twenty watts. He quickly outgrew this arrangement, however. The U.S. Department of Commerce granted his radio station, WLW, license #312 on March 2, 1922. In 1923, Crosley established the Crosley Radio Corporation.

At one point, WLW was the most powerful radio station in the world, with an experimental license to broadcast at 500,000 watts. It was truly "the big one," as it is frequently called. President Franklin Delano Roosevelt flipped a gold-plated telegraph switch in the White House, turning on the power of those 50kW. However, he might just as well have flipped the switch that lifted the floodgates of complaints. Radio stations in Canada and upstate New York immediately complained to the Federal Communications Commission that their signals were being obliterated by WLW's. As a result, WLW was limited to broadcasting at 50,000 watts during the daytime for regular broadcasting. The FCC license card was then amended as follows: "Modification of special experimental authorization to use 500 kw [*sic*] power from local sunset to 6 A.M. using directional antenna to reduce signal in Niagara to Lockport N.Y. area to equivalent of 50 kw for period ending 8-1-35."

About that same time, a woman by the name of Ruth Lyons worked for a competing Cincinnati radio station, WKRC. Her first on-air gig came when a female radio host called in sick. Lyons was asked to fill in, and a star was born. She became the host of her own afternoon show on WKRC.

Her short career with WKRC still had its highlights. During the horrendous Cincinnati flood of 1937, she broadcast nonstop—both to provide comfort and to seek donations. A less traumatic and yet less-known achievement reflected her musical talent. Every week, she composed a new song to perform while accompanying herself on the piano.

In 1942, when WKRC would not give her a ten-dollar raise, Lyons left for WLW and WSAI. (It is widely acknowledged that WKRC's unwillingness to pay the extra ten dollars cost them millions.) On WLW, she hosted *Petticoat Partyline* and, later, *WLW Consumer's Foundation*. Lyons's magnum opus was *The 50 Club*, created in 1949. It was so named for the fifty lucky women attending the daily luncheon and broadcast. In the 1950s, because of incredible response, the luncheon was expanded to fill two studios, and the show was renamed *The 50-50 Club*. By then, the show was being simultaneously broadcast on WLW radio and WLWT-TV, NBC's first affiliate outside of the East Coast. The show was carried by NBC nationally for eleven months of 1951 and was broadcast in color in 1957 by WLWT. It remained on the air with Ruth Lyons as the host until her retirement in January 1967, at which time her "sidekick" Bob Braun took over.

Lyons's word was golden: one mention of an advertiser's product and the merchandise would fly off the shelves. Sponsors waited more than a year to get *advertising* time. People waited up to five years to get tickets to be in the audience. When the City of Cincinnati held a "Ruth Lyons Day" in 1957, more than 100,000 people had to be turned away.

"People came from as far as California," said Dorothy Kuhn, one of Lyons's assistants for the show. "If they got tickets, they had them in their wills!" Some of Kuhn's most cherished memories were when Lyons would just sit down at the piano in the studio and play. "She was an incredible person," Kuhn added, saying that the show was the love of her life. "And she knew *everything* about the business. Ruth Lyons was personally responsible for our progress at Channel 5."[95]

Kuhn noted that the luncheon part of the show had to be discontinued to accommodate more people. "It got too large," explained Kuhn. The audience members didn't go unfed, however. "What people might not know is that Bob [Braun] had a restaurant down on Fourth Street. When the buses of people came in, I would book them down there."

In the world of television talk shows, certain names stand out as the forerunners of their slot: Steve Allen at night, Tom Snyder for late night, Mike Douglas (in Cleveland in 1961) and Phil Donahue (in Dayton in 1967) for daytime—even Chris Hardwick for the zombie apocalypse. However, it

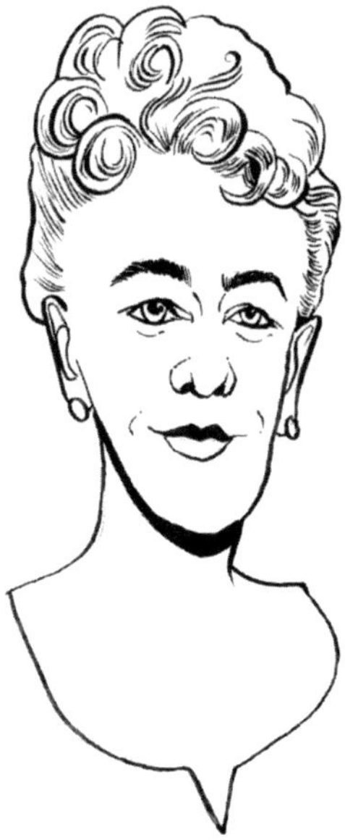

Ruth Lyons was a beloved figure in Cincinnati radio and television. *Illustration by Allison Ranieri.*

could be argued that all these shows owe their existence to Ruth Lyons. Oprah Winfrey, the queen of daytime TV, wrote in September 2002 in *O, The Oprah Magazine*, "If there had been no Phil Donahue, there would be no Oprah Winfrey Show." Donahue himself told *Chicago Tribune* writer Bob Greene in 1988, "If there had not been a Crosley Broadcasting with a commitment to local programming, and if there had not been a Ruth Lyons, I probably wouldn't be here."[96]

However, Ruth Lyons's life was not all white gloves and roses. In 1944, she and her husband, Herman Newman (a professor of English at the University of Cincinnati), adopted a little girl named Candace. Candy became a fixture on her mother's show. The three enjoyed life, going on many cruises as a family. Two things marred this idyllic existence: in December 1964, Lyons suffered a stroke. One month later, Candy found a lump in her breast. Surgery followed immediately at Holmes Hospital, followed by treatment for the cancer. By February 1966, Candy's cancer was clearly winning, so the family decided to go on one more cruise. They boarded the SS *Michelangelo* on June 3, 1966, for a trip to Europe. One last cruise was not to be. Candy got gravely ill en route and had to be hospitalized in Italy. After her treatment, they boarded the ship for home but didn't make it. On the evening of Father's Day, June 19, 1966, she died peacefully around 10:00 p.m. (Although hideous rumors circulated for years that she jumped overboard, this is not the case.) Candy was cremated in New York and is interred with her parents at the Hillside Crematorium in Cincinnati.[97]

Even years before this tragedy, Ruth Lyons was devoted to children. In a visit to Cincinnati's Children's Hospital, she noticed that the children didn't have enough toys to play with. At Christmastime, she began a drive to collect toys for children who were hospitalized for the holidays. The Ruth Lyons Children's Christmas Fund was born in 1939. Lyons's whole staff worked on the fund.

"Ruth would schedule us even in the evenings, when we were supposed to be off," Kuhn recalled. "We'd meet in her private office, with its rocking chairs, and she would order us dinner. We would make calls asking for gifts and sponsors." Finally, the fund grew too large and was turned over to the bank for control. But that didn't remove Lyons from participating personally. "She'd go to the hospital herself with teddy bears, dollies and other toys," said Kuhn.

After almost eighty years, the Ruth Lyons Children's Fund (renamed in 1996) is still going strong, assisting the Division of Child Life at Cincinnati Children's Hospital Medical Center, one of the leading pediatric hospitals in the nation. Many of today's Cincinnati families have been touched by the kindness of Ruth Lyons. She was truly one of Cincinnati's wonders.

NOTES

Introduction

1. History.com staff, "Seven Wonders of the Ancient World," History.com, published 2009, accessed October 18, 2016, www.history.com/topics/ancient-history/sevens-wonders-of-the-ancient-world.
2. Matt Rosenberg, "The Seven Wonders of the World," About.com, accessed October 18, 2016, geography.about.com/od/lists/a/sevenwonders.htm.

Chapter 1

3. Society for the Preservation of Music Hall, "Bones Discovered Under Music Hall," www.spmhcincinnati.org/Music-Hall-History/Skeletons-and-Bones.php.
4. Steven Rosen, "Digging Up the Past for Future Development," Soapbox Cincinnati, March 29, 2011, www.soapboxmedia.com/features/0329graypapecincinnati.aspx.
5. R.A. Davis, "Building Stones in the Vicinity of Fountain Square, Cincinnati Ohio: A Walking Tour in Celebration of Earth Science Week 2000," American Institute of Professional Geologists, Ohio Department of Natural Resources Division of Geological Survey, the College of Mount St. Joseph, October 14, 2000, accessed January 23, 2017, geosurvey.ohiodnr.gov/portals/geosurvey/PDFs/Tours_Walking_Driving/cinctour.pdf.
6. Pender, *100 Things to Do in Cincinnati*, 104.

7. City of Cincinnati, "Major Architectural Styles," accessed January 23, 2017, www.cincinnati-oh.gov/buildings/historic-conservation/major-architectural-styles.
8. Supreme Court of Ohio and the Ohio Judicial System, "Potter Stewart (Jan. 23, 1915–Dec. 7, 1985)," accessed June 5, 2017, www.supremecourt.ohio.gov/MJC/places/pStewart.asp.
9. Robert W. Rydell, "World's Columbian Exposition," Encyclopedia of Chicago, accessed June 13, 2017, www.encyclopedia.chicagohistory.org/pages/1386.html.
10. Phil Armstrong, "Cincy Through the Decades: 150 Years of Architectural History," May 16, 2016, accessed March 23, 2017, cincinnatirefined.com/travel/cincinnati-through-the-decades-150-years-of-building-in-the-urban-core.
11. Paul A. Tenkotte, "Our Rich History: Appreciating Those Fascinating Skyscrapers, Offering Treasure Trove of Views, History," *Northern Kentucky Tribune*, July 20, 2015, accessed March 23, 2017, www.nkytribune.com/2015/07/our-rich-history-appreciating-those-fascinating-skyscrapers-offering-treasure-trove-of-views-history.
12. Davis, "Building Stones in the Vicinity of Fountain Square."
13. Joseph J. Korom, *The American Skyscraper, 1850–1940: A Celebration of Height* (Wellesley, MA: Branden Books, 2008), accessed June 14, 2017, books.google.com/books?id=JVzYO1TyZ6AC&dq=The+American+Skyscraper,+1850-1940:+A+Celebration+of+Height&source=gbs_navlinks_s, 308.
14. Tenkotte, "Our Rich History."
15. Davis, "Building Stones in the Vicinity of Fountain Square."
16. Contemporary Arts Center, accessed May 24, 2017, www.contemporaryartscenter.org/about.
17. Contemporary Arts Center, accessed May 24, 2017, www.contemporaryartscenter.org/exhibitions/2015/11/after-the-moment.
18. Herbert Muschamp, "ART/ARCHITECTURE: Zaha Hadid's Urban Mothership," *New York Times*, June 8, 2003, accessed June 14, 2017, www.nytimes.com/2003/06/08/arts/art-architecture-zaha-hadid-s-urban-mothership.html.
19. Mary Niehaus, "The Renewal of Campus," *UC Magazine, University of Cincinnati*, June 2001, accessed April 13, 2017, magazine.uc.edu/issues/0601/master-plan.html.
20. Deborah Rieselman, "Tourist Guide to UC: 80 Sights Not to Miss, Plus 5 that Can't Be Seen," *UC Magazine, University of Cincinnati*, July 2014, accessed February 16, 2017, magazine.uc.edu/issues/0714/openingStory.html.

21. The Great American Stations (Amtrak), "Cincinnati OH," copyright 2016, accessed June 3, 2017, www.greatamericanstations.com/stations/cincinnati-oh-cin.

Chapter 2

22. Beckman, *Founders and Famous Families*, 138–39.
23. Pender, *100 Things to Do in Cincinnati*, 86.
24. Abby S. Schwartz, "Nicholas Longworth: Art Patron of Cincinnati," *Cincinnati Museum Center*, Spring 1988, accessed June 2, 2017, library.cincymuseum.org/topics/l/files/longworth/qch-v46-n1-nic-017.pdf.
25. D.H. Jacques, *The Rural Carolinian: The Great Southern Illustrated Agricultural Magazine Published by Walker, Evans & Cogswell and D. Wyatt Aiken*, 1871, books.google.com/books?id=EjwyVVQ818UC60.
26. Beckman, *Founders and Famous Families*, 137.
27. Taft Museum of Art, "Museum History," accessed May 28, 2017, www.taftmuseum.org/museumhistory.
28. Beckman, *Founders and Famous Families*, 156–57.
29. Cincinnati Ballet, "Mission & History," accessed May 25, 2017, www.cballet.org/mission-history.
30. David Lyman, "Cincinnati Ballet at 50: 50 Fun Facts," Cincinnati.com, February 27, 2014, accessed May 26, 2017, www.cincinnati.com/picture-gallery/entertainment/2014/02/27/cincinnati-ballet-at-50-50-fun-facts/5858689.
31. Pender, *100 Things to Do in Cincinnati*, 84.
32. David Lyman, "Playhouse in the Park to Get New Home, but on Same Site," *Cincinnati Enquirer*, February 16, 2017, accessed April 24, 2017, www.cincinnati.com/story/entertainment/theater/2017/02/16/playhouse-park-get-new-home-but-same-site/97914356.
33. American Sign Museum, "Take a Walk Down Memory Lane," accessed June 3, 2017, www.americansignmuseum.org/about.

Chapter 3

34. Beckman, *Founders and Famous Families*, 143.
35. Ibid., 88.
36. Ibid., 95.

37. Ibid., 96–97.
38. Bowdeya Tweh and Carrie Blackmore Smith, "Rookwood Pottery CEO Wade Exits Role," *Cincinnati Enquirer*, April 29, 2015, accessed June 2, 2017, www.cincinnati.com/story/money/2015/04/28/rookwood-owner-exits/26496487.
39. *Annual Report, Public Library of Cincinnati and Hamilton County*, 2015.
40. Telephone interview with author, April 21, 2017.
41. E-mail to author, April 27, 2017.

Chapter 4

42. Kathy Reed, "The Island Queen and Coney Island," A River Runs Through Us blog, April 13, 2012, accessed June 14, 2017, ohioriverways.blogspot.com/2012/04/island-queen-and-coney-island.html?showComment=1497450872705#c1912383729446514745.
43. Pender, *100 Things to Do in Cincinnati*, 23.
44. Don Prout, "Coney Island," Cincinnati Views blog, accessed June 14, 2017, www.cincinnativiews.net/coney_island_main.htm.
45. Oktoberfest Zinzinnati, "About Oktoberfest," accessed June 1, 2017, www.oktoberfestzinzinnati.com/About/About_Oktoberfest.aspx.
46. Pender, *100 Things to Do in Cincinnati*, 62.
47. Cincinnati Zoo and Botanical Garden, "Festival of Lights," accessed June 11, 2017, cincinnatizoo.org/events/festival-of-lights.
48. CPFansite blog, "Kings Island History," 2013, accessed June 4, 2017, cpfansite.com/kifansite/kings-island-history.
49. Pender, *100 Things to Do in Cincinnati*, 70.

Chapter 5

50. Beckman, *Founders and Famous Families*, 108.
51. Ibid., 111.
52. Ibid., 112.
53. Dann Woellert, "Jets and Sharks and Aglamesis Ice Cream," dannwoellertthefoodetymologist, March 25, 2017, accessed March 27, 2017, dannwoellertthefoodetymologist.wordpress.com/2017/03/25/jets-and-sharks-and-aglamesis-ice-cream/comment-page-1.
54. Beckman, *Founders and Famous Families*, 113.

55. Ibid., 114.
56. Alyssa Brandt, "The Man Who Came to Dinner," *Cincinnati Magazine*, November 27, 2013, accessed May 29, 2017, www.cincinnatimagazine.com/features/the-man-who-came-to-dinner.
57. Julie Irwin Zimmerman, "The Benefactor," *Cincinnati Magazine*, September 1, 2011, accessed March 21, 2017, www.cincinnatimagazine.com/features/the-benefactor3.
58. Findlay Market, "A Brief History," accessed June 3, 2017, www.findlaymarket.org/history.
59. Findlay Market, "Findlay Market Merchants," accessed June 3, 2017, www.findlaymarket.org/market-merchants.
60. E-mail from Matt Ewer to author, May 26, 2017.
61. Beckman, *Founders and Famous Families*, 72.
62. Jim Siegel, "Ohio Lawmakers Seek to Loosen Regulations on Craft Breweries, Distilleries," *Columbus Dispatch*, May 2, 2016, accessed June 4, 2017, www.dispatch.com/content/stories/local/2016/05/02/lawmakers-look-to-loosen-regulations-on-craft-breweries-distilleries.html.
63. Personal conversation with author, April 16, 2009.
64. Rita Nader Heikenfeld, "The Great Goetta Debate," About Eating.com from Rita Nader Heikenfeld blog, 2013, accessed April 26, 2017, abouteating.com/goetta-recipes.
65. Dann Woellert, "A Mispronounced German Delicacy," The Food Etymologist blog, August 5, 2014, accessed April 11, 2017, dannwoellertthefoodetymologist.wordpress.com/2014/08/05/a-mispronounced-german-delicacy.

Chapter 6

66. Beckman, *Founders and Famous Families*, 105.
67. Silberstein, *Cincinnati Then and Now*, 47.
68. Beckman, *Founders and Famous Families*, 45.
69. Cincinnati Parks, "Welcome to Cincinnati Parks," June 4, 2017, www.cincinnatiparks.com.
70. Beckman, *Founders and Famous Families*, 1–2.
71. National Park Service, "John Quincy Adams," www.nps.gov/adam/index.htm.
72. My aunt (by marriage to my mother's oldest brother) is ninety-six-year-old Katherine Jermain Porter Felmeth. Her grandfather was Charles

F. Porter, youngest brother of Jermain Gildersleeve Porter, director of the Cincinnati Observatory from 1884 to 1930. Jermain Gildersleeve Porter had two sons, John Jermain (who taught chemistry at UC even while he was earning his own bachelor's degree) and Harold Mitchel (named for Ormsby Macknight Mitchel), who also studied chemistry at UC. Incidentally, Jermain's two sons (John and Harold) invented the Chemcraft chemistry kits that thrilled kids and scared their parents from 1916 to the 1960s.

73. Cincinnati Observatory, accessed June 14, 2017, www.cincinnatiobservatory.org/about.

74. Beckman, *Founders and Famous Families*, 3.

75. Kathy S. Koops, "Where Are the Seven Hills in Cincinnati?" CincyBlog, November 19, 2010, accessed June 14, 2017, thecincyblog.com/2010/11/19/where-are-the-seven-hills-in-cincinnati.

76. Greg Hand, "How Many Hills Does Cincinnati Have?" Cincinnati Curiosities blog, 2015, accessed June 14, 2017, handeaux.tumblr.com/post/118436745717/how-many-hills-does-cincinnati-have-it-turns-out.

Chapter 7

77. Beckman, *Founders and Famous Families*, 122.

78. Ibid., 149.

79. Ibid., 120.

80. Ibid., 67.

81. Harlow, *Serene Cincinnatians*, 210.

82. Beckman, *Founders and Famous Families*, 60–61.

83. Nuxhall, *Beauty in the Grove*, xv.

84. Spring Grove Cemetery and Arboretum, accessed June 15, 2017, www.springgrove.org/about.aspx.

85. Pender, *100 Things to Do in Cincinnati*, 88.

86. Herman Lackman Brewing Company, accessed March 25, 2017, www.lightoverglass.com/the_lackman_building.html.

Chapter 8

87. Beckman, *Founders and Famous Families*, 51.

88. Wendy Hart Beckman, "The Lazarus Family: Sold on the City," *Cincinnati Magazine*, November 2014, www.cincinnatimagazine.com/citywiseblog/lazarus-sold-city.
89. Beckman, *Founders and Famous Families*, 124–26.
90. SPACE.com staff, "Neil Armstrong: First Man on the Moon," August 25, 2013, accessed May 29, 2017, www.space.com/15519-neil-armstrong-man-moon.html.
91. Jeff Suess, "175-Year-Old Emery Chemical Company Turned Lard into Largesse," October 8, 2015, accessed March 25, 2017, www.cincinnati.com.
92. Beckman, *Founders and Famous Families*, 93.
93. Ibid., 129.
94. Interview with author, August 2009.
95. Telephone interview with author, March 13, 2017.
96. Bob Greene, "A TV Legend Who Didn't Talk Trash," *Chicago Tribune*, November 15, 1988, accessed March 15, 2017, articles.chicagotribune.com/1988-11-15/features/8802160677_1_trash-television-audience-ruth-lyons.
97. Mike Martini, "Let's Put a Painful Father's Day Story to Bed," *Cincinnati Enquirer*, June 19, 2016, accessed March 13, 2017, www.cincinnati.com/story/opinion/contributors/2016/06/19/lets-put-painful-fathers-day-story-bed/85920072.

BIBLIOGRAPHY

Banks, Michael A. *Before Oprah: Ruth Lyons, the Woman Who Created Talk TV*. Wilmington, OH: Orange Frazer Press, 2009.

Beckman, Wendy Hart. *Founders and Famous Families of Cincinnati*. Covington, KY: Clerisy Press, 2014.

Bellman, Sacha DeVroomen, and Felix Winternitz. *Insider's Guide to Cincinnati*. Guilford, CT: Globe Pequot Press, 2009.

Grace, Kevin. *Legendary Locals of Cincinnati*. Charleston, SC: Arcadia Publishing, 2011.

Harlow, Alvin F. *The Serene Cincinnatians (Society in America Series)*. New York: E.P. Dutton and Company, Inc., 1950.

Horstman, Barry M. *100 Who Made a Difference: Greater Cincinnatians Who Made a Mark on the 20th Century*. Cincinnati, OH: Cincinnati Post, 1999.

Moore, Gina Ruffin. *Cincinnati*. Chicago: Arcadia Publishing, 2007.

Morgan, Michael D. *Over-the-Rhine: When Beer Was King*. Charleston, SC: The History Press, 2010.

Nuxhall, Phil. *Beauty in the Grove: Spring Grove Cemetery & Arboretum*. Wilmington, OH: Orange Frazer Press, 2009.

Pender, Rick. *100 Things to Do in Cincinnati Before You Die*. St. Louis: Reedy Press, LLC, 2016.

Perry, Dick. *Vas You Ever in Zinzinnati?* New York: Doubleday & Co., 1966.

Ranker. "List of Famous Buildings & Structures." www.ranker.com/list/cincinnati-buildings-and-structures/reference (accessed January 23, 2017).

Rolfes, Steven J. *Cincinnati Landmarks*. Charleston, SC: Arcadia Publishing, 2012.

Silberstein, Iola Hessler. *Cincinnati Then and Now*. Cincinnati, OH: League of Women Voters, 1982.

Smiddy, Betty Ann, with support of the Public Library of Cincinnati and Hamilton County. *Cincinnati's Great Disasters*. Chicago: Arcadia Publishing, 2007.

Smiddy, Betty Ann, with the photography of Frank Wilmes. *Cincinnati's Golden Age*. Charleston, SC: Arcadia Publishing, 2005.

Tolzmann, Don. *Over-the-Rhine Tour Guide: Cincinnati's Historic German District, Over-the-Rhine, and Environs*. Milford, OH: Little Miami Publishing Co., 2011.

Writers' Program of the Work Projects Administration in the State of Ohio. *Cincinnati: A Guide to the Queen City and Its Neighbors*. Cincinnati, OH: Wiesen-Hart Press, 1943.

Other good resources, if you're interested in the region:

Cincinnati Enquirer

Cincinnati Magazine

Fanfare, the magazine of the Cincinnati Symphony and Pops Orchestra

UC Magazine

INDEX

J

K

L

M

N

O

P

ABOUT THE AUTHOR AND ILLUSTRATOR

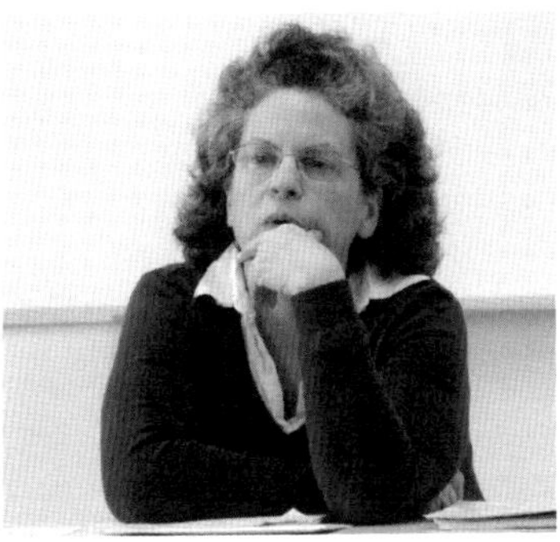

Wendy Hart Beckman is an award-winning freelance writer and editor. Her seventh and eighth books, published in 2014, are *Founders and Famous Families of Cincinnati* and *University of Cincinnati College of Nursing: 125 Years of Transforming Health Care*, respectively. She has also published about three hundred articles in print and online publications and has received a baker's dozen of awards for her writing, editing and desktop publishing. She is currently working on a novel set in the 1980s.

Wendy's bachelor's degrees are in geology and natural science/technical communications from Virginia Tech and the University of Cincinnati. She has a master's degree in English and a graduate certificate in professional writing from UC. Wendy has taught business, scientific and technical writing at the University of Cincinnati and cultural diversity at Miami University. She tutors high school kids in reading, writing, science and English. For adult writers who wish to get published, she holds many workshops each year, from a few hours in length to weekend-long retreats.

She is the mother of three sons, wife to Steve and grandmother to one adorable granddaughter.

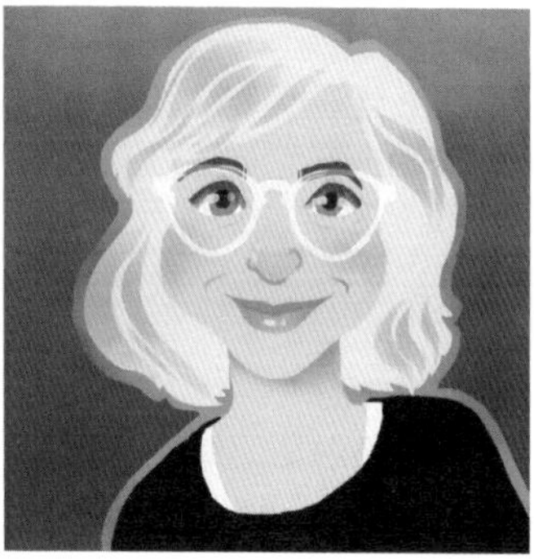

Allison Ranieri is a Cincinnati native working hard to patronize all of the area breweries, discover all of the beautiful nature of Ohio she's never seen, draw a lot and draw every day and generally be a better human being than the day before. You can find her giving creative advice and sharing her process on YouTube.